Sashiko
and Beyond

Sashiko
and Beyond

Techniques and projects
for quilting
in the Japanese style

Saikoh Takano

Chilton Book Company
Radnor, Pennsylvania

Acknowledgements

I would like to express my grateful thanks to the following people, without whose help this book would not have been possible. My thanks go to my British friends, Mrs Barbara Janssen, who worked the *houou* design on pages 64-5, and Mrs Pamela McDowall, who worked the *ougi* design on pages 66-7, and to my Dutch friend, Mrs H.J. de Haas-Siertsema, who worked the waistcoat on pages 104-7.

My thanks also go to Bundai Sadako, Hachiya Junko, Iizuka Mitsuko, Kakuta Hatsuko, Kawakami Reiko, Kawazura Fusako, Minami Kimiko, Mori Fumiko, Murakami Naoko, Nakanishi Chie, Satoh Syoh, Takahashi Mistuko, Takahashi Yae, Takasaki Kikuko, Takenaka Chizuko, Takizawa Takako and Tomioka Yasuko.

The photographs for this book were taken by Yusai Fukuyama.

First published 1993
Reprinted 1995

First published in the United States in
Radnor, Pennsylvania
by Chilton Book Company

Typeset by Express Typesetting Ltd

Printed in Singapore

Published by
B.T. Batsford Ltd
4 Fitzhardinge Street
London W1H 0AH

British Library cataloguing-in-publication data.
A catalogue record for this book is available from the British Library.

ISBN 0-8019-8514-5

Contents

Introduction

The Japanese word *sashiko* means 'little stabs', or running stitch. Originally this simple stitch was used as a practical technique to quilt together several layers of loosely woven fabric for strength and warmth. Early fabrics were made from grass, tree-bark fibres, ramie or silk, but in the fifteenth century cotton was introduced to Japan, where it flourished in the warm southern climate. In the north, hemp is still grown especially for *sashiko*. Decorative *sashiko* developed during the eighteenth century, when there was increased prosperity in Japan and cheap cotton fabrics were readily available.

During the second half of the Edo period, private fire brigades were established in Tokyo.

Sashiko was used for the firemen's protective coats, which were drenched with water before they fought a fire. The decorated side was designed to be worn on the inside, except on special occasions, and the patterns often included dragons or warlike human figures. Examples of nineteenth- and early twentieth-century coats can be seen in the Victoria and Albert Museum in London, and in folk museums in Japan.

Different areas of Japan have each developed their own distinctive *sashiko* techniques and patterns. *Sashiko* is also often used in combination with patchwork or appliqué to create more complex designs. For example, the Ainu people of Hokkaido Island produce bold, flowing water patterns in intricately worked quilted appliqué, which they overstitch with chain stitch (see pages 70-1).

In recent years, there has been a revival of interest in these traditional techniques in Japan, as there has been in many Western countries. Modern *sashiko* designs include the traditional geometric patterns, worked in white stitching on indigo-dyed fabric, as well as figurative images of trees and flowers.

I am delighted to be able to introduce these techniques to readers outside Japan, and to show them some of the many ideas for different designs.

Saikoh Takano
Tokyo, 1992

Opposite: **Sayagata** *(Buddhist symbol). The method of working is illustrated on page 24.*

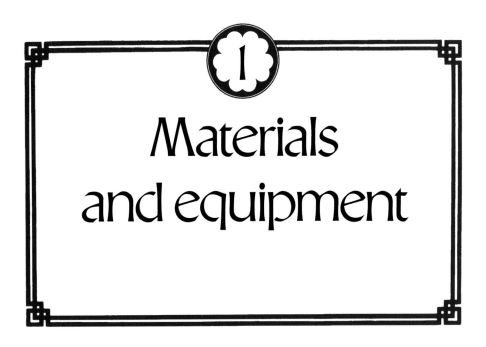

Materials and equipment

Fabrics

Traditional *sashiko* quilting is worked on indigo-dyed fabric, but any smooth, soft, plain-coloured fabric can be used. Cotton, linen, crêpe de Chine and satin are all suitable.

The fabrics used in patchwork should be the same weight; if the finished piece is to be washable, you will also need to use the same type of fabric, for example, all cotton.

The backing fabric should be the same weight as the top fabric, or finer.

Pre-wash all washable fabrics and test for colourfastness. If the colour runs, soak the fabric in five parts cold water to one part vinegar. Iron the fabric, straightening the grain as you do so.

Opposite: **Shippou** (Seven treasures). *The method of working this traditional design is illustrated on page 30.*

Interlining

This is not traditionally used in *sashiko* quilting, but if you wish to make the finished item warmer or thicker you can insert a layer of wadding between the top fabric and the backing. Synthetic wadding is normally used as it is easy to stitch through and dries quickly when washed. It is available in different weights; 70 g (2 oz) is the weight used for most of the projects in this book.

Sewing equipment

Frames
An embroidery frame can be useful, especially if you are couching with gold thread.

A frame clamped to a table or floor stand is recommended.

Threads
The choice of threads depends very much on the fabric and the design. For *sashiko* quilting, a soft, twisted, fine cotton thread (no. 6) or *coton à broder* is normally used. For patchwork, use cotton threads no. 50 or 60, in colours to match the fabrics.

Surface embroidery can be worked in stranded cotton or *coton perlé*.

Needles
Choose appropriate needles for the particular fabrics and threads you are using, selecting those with which you feel comfortable.

Pins
Fine dressmaker's pins or lacemaker's pins are recommended for medium-weight or fine fabrics. For heavier-weight fabrics, use larger pins with coloured heads so that they do not become 'lost' in the fabric.

Thimble
Even if you do not normally use a thimble, you will probably find that you need one to push the needle through layers of quilting.

Scissors
You will need a large pair of scissors for cutting out fabric, a small pair of needlework scissors when you are stitching, and a separate pair of scissors for cutting paper.

Designing equipment

○ tissue paper
○ ruler
○ French chalk, tailor's chalk or coloured pencils
○ dressmaker's carbon paper
○ dressmaker's tracing wheel or Japanese *hera* (a knife-shaped tool made of bone)
○ pair of compasses, set square and protractor
○ tracing paper
○ graph paper and isometric graph paper

Fig. 1

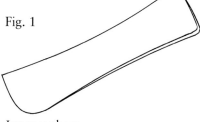

Japanese hera.

Techniques

Methods of working

Transferring the design

There are several methods of transferring designs to the fabric:

1. For simple repeat designs, draw the design directly on the fabric, using a template and French chalk, tailor's chalk or a water-erasable pen.

2. Draw a geometric design directly on the right side (RS) of the fabric, using tailor's chalk and a ruler.

3. Trace the design on paper and pin to the right side of the fabric, with dressmaker's carbon paper between the paper and the fabric. Outline the design with a dressmaker's wheel, a *hera* or a sharply pointed pencil (fig. 2a).

4. For thick woollen fabrics, trace the design on tissue paper and pin to the right side of the fabric. Stitch round the outline of the design in small tacking stitches, using a contrast-colour thread (fig. 2b), then carefully tear away the tissue paper. Remove the tacking stitches after the work is completed.

Tacking the layers together

1. Lay the backing fabric wrong side (WS) up on a flat surface. Place the wadding (if required) on top and then the top fabric, right side up.

2. Tack horizontal rows of stitches to hold the three layers in place, working from the centre outwards. Then tack vertical lines of stitching.

Sashiko

As well as being used in quilting, *sashiko* designs can be worked on top of patchwork and with appliqué, or as embroidery on a single layer of fabric.

Fig. 2a   *A design outlined with a dressmaker's wheel.*

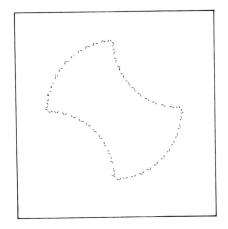

Fig. 2b   *The outline of the same design transferred to the fabric by stitching through tissue paper.*

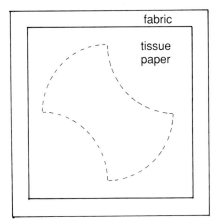

Sashiko quilting can be worked through two layers, a top fabric and a backing fabric, or with the addition of wadding sandwiched between, making three layers in all. In either case, the finished piece of work can also be lined with a further layer of lining fabric.

To enlarge or reduce the size of a design, transfer it to larger or smaller graph paper square by square, or make your own graph paper.

How to start
Make a knot at the end of the thread and start stitching with the knot hidden in the backing fabric. Alternatively, secure the thread by making a few small stitches from the starting point and then stitching back again.

Joining threads
Bring the new thread up from the back of the work a few stitches before the end of the previous line of sewing. Stitch along the existing stitches to secure the thread.

a

To move from one part of the design to another, slide the needle along underneath the backing fabric, making a small stitch at intervals.

b

If the work is reversible, slide the needle along between the top and backing fabric so that the thread will not show on the other side.

Fig. 4

Finishing
At the end of a line of stitching, work back a few small stitches to secure the thread.

Tension
It is important to keep an even tension throughout your work. Tight stitching will pucker the fabric, and loose stitching does not look professional. If there is a sharp curve in the design, or a long line of straight stitching, make a small loop of thread under the backing fabric or between the two fabrics if the work is to be reversible (fig. 3). This will prevent the stitching from shrinking and puckering when the work is washed.

When you want to move from one part of the design to another, slide the needle along underneath the backing fabric and make a small stitch at intervals (fig. 4a). If the work is to be reversible, slide the needle along between the top and backing fabrics so that the thread will be invisible (fig. 4b).

Fig. 3 *Make small loops of thread in long lines of straight stitching and at sharp corners.*

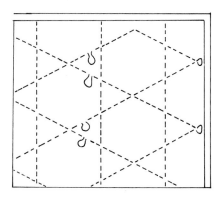

The front and back of the same piece of sashiko *work.*

Stitches
Traditionally only running stitch was used for sashiko, but other stitches can also be used:

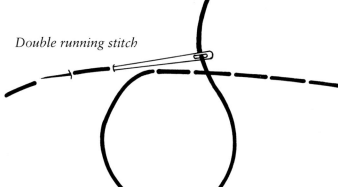

Double running stitch

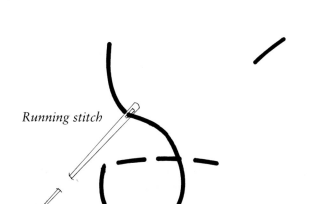

Running stitch

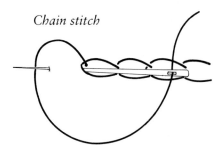

Chain stitch

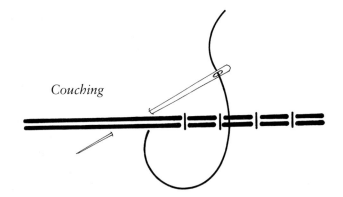

Couching

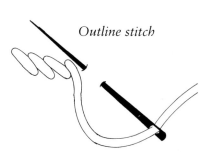

Outline stitch

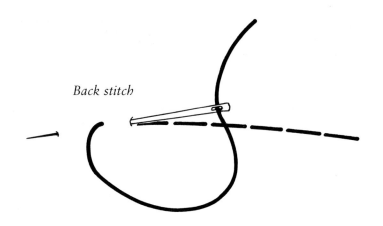

Back stitch

French knot

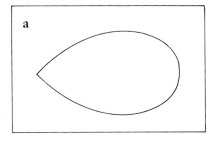

Transfer the design to the RS of the appliqué fabric (see page 11).

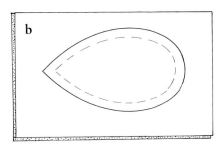

Position the appliqué fabric on the background fabric and tack inside the outline of the motif.

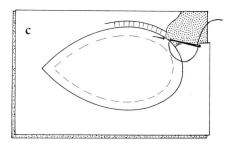

Cut round the edge of the motif. Turn under the seam allowance and slipstitch.

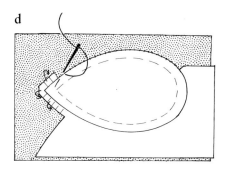

To *turn a corner, fold under the seam allowance as shown.*

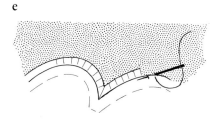

To *stitch round a curve or flower shape, clip into the seam allowance almost to the edge of the outline.*

Fig. 5

Appliqué

1. Transfer the motif to the right side of the appliqué fabric, using one of the methods described on page 11 (fig. 5a).

2. Lay the background fabric RS up on a flat surface. Position the appliqué fabric on top, RS uppermost. Pin the two layers of fabric together. Tack round the edge of the appliqué motif, 5 mm (¼ in) inside the outline (fig. 5b).

3. Cut round the edge of the motif, 3-4 mm (⅛ in) outside the outline. (The seam allowance will vary according to the thickness of the fabric, and whether the motif is curved or not.) Clip the curves, if necessary. Turn under the seam allowance, using

the point of a needle. Slipstitch round the outline of the motif (fig. 5c).

4. If the motif has a sharp corner or point, fold under the seam allowance as shown (fig. 5d). Make a small stitch to hold, stitch as normal to the point, fold, and then continue stitching.

5. For a flower shape or any other awkward curve, clip into the seam allowance almost to the edge of the outline. Turn under the seam, using the point of a needle, and hold in place with your first and second fingers. Slipstitch carefully in place, then stitch the other side of the curve in the same way (fig. 5e).

Reverse appliqué

In this case, transfer the motif to the RS of the *background* fabric, using one of the methods described on page 11.

Lay the reverse-appliqué fabric on a flat surface, RS up. Lay the background fabric on top. Pin and then tack the two fabrics together, stitching 5 mm (¼ in) outside the outline of the motif (fig. 6).

Cut the background fabric inside the outline of the motif, leaving a 5 mm (¼ in) seam allowance. Use small, sharp scissors and only cut a little way at a time to prevent cutting the layer of fabric underneath (fig. 7a, overleaf). It may be easier if you lift the top fabric

Fig. 6

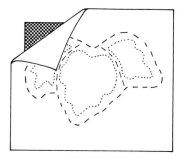

Lay the background fabric on to the reverse-appliqué fabric. Tack outside the outline of the motif.

Using small scissors, cut the background fabric inside the outline of the motif.

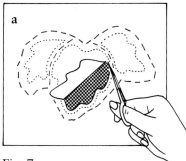

Fig. 7

with a pin. Clip the curves, if necessary.

Turn under the seam allowance, using a needle. (For a neater seam of 3 mm (⅛ in), use PVA adhesive to hold the

Fig. 8

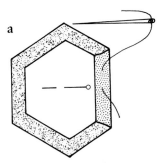

Pin the paper shape to the WS of the fabric shape. Fold under the first edge of fabric and tack.

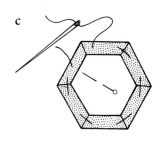

At the final corner, slip the last edge under the first.

Turn under the seam allowance and slipstitch.

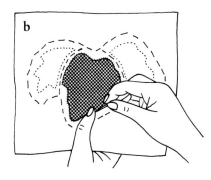

turned-under edges in place.) Slipstitch round the edge of the motif (fig. 7b).

Turn the fabric over and cut away the excess seam allowance to leave a neat edge.

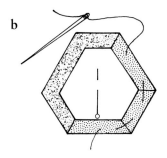

Fold under each edge of fabric in turn and tack in place.

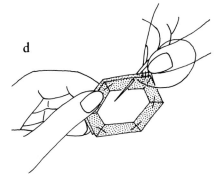

Place two patches RS together and oversew along the edge.

Patchwork

Trace the patchwork shape and make a template from thick card or plastic. Cut as many shapes as are needed from paper, to the exact size of the template, taking care to be very accurate. Cut the same number of shapes from fabric, this time allowing a 5-8 mm (¼–⅜ in) seam allowance all round. (The seam allowance will vary according to the thickness of the fabric.)

To make a patch, lay the fabric shape on a flat surface, WS uppermost. Place the paper shape in the centre and pin. Fold the fabric (the seam allowance) over one side of the paper shape and tack (fig. 8a). Fold the second edge and tack, and so on (fig. 8b). At the final corner, slip the last seam allowance under the first, tack in place (fig. 8c) and then work back one or two stitches to secure the thread.

To join the patches together, place them RS together. Using matching thread, oversew along the edge (fig. 8d). Do not knot the end of the thread, but start stitching 5 mm (¼ in) from a corner and then stitch back over the thread to secure. Continue adding extra patches to make up the design (fig. 8e).

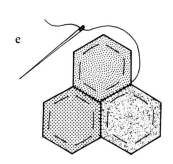

Add extra patches to make up the design.

Sashiko designs

Kagome (Basketweave)

This design is taken from the hexagonal pattern on woven bamboo baskets.

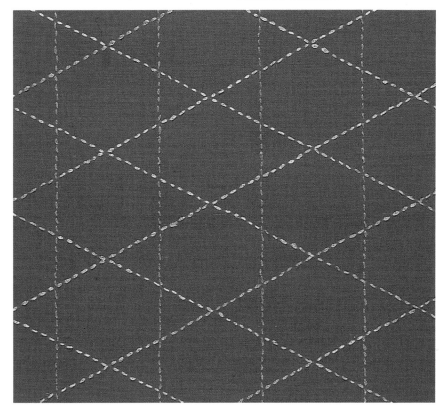

Basketweave, from which this pattern takes its name.

Designing
Use any size of graph paper. Draw diagonal and vertical lines as shown.

Order of working
Work outwards from the centre of the design. Stitch the vertical lines first, and then the diagonal lines.

Designing

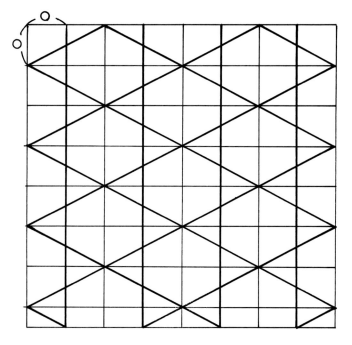

Order of working

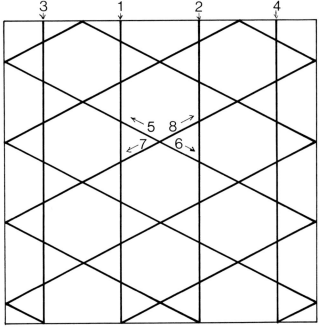

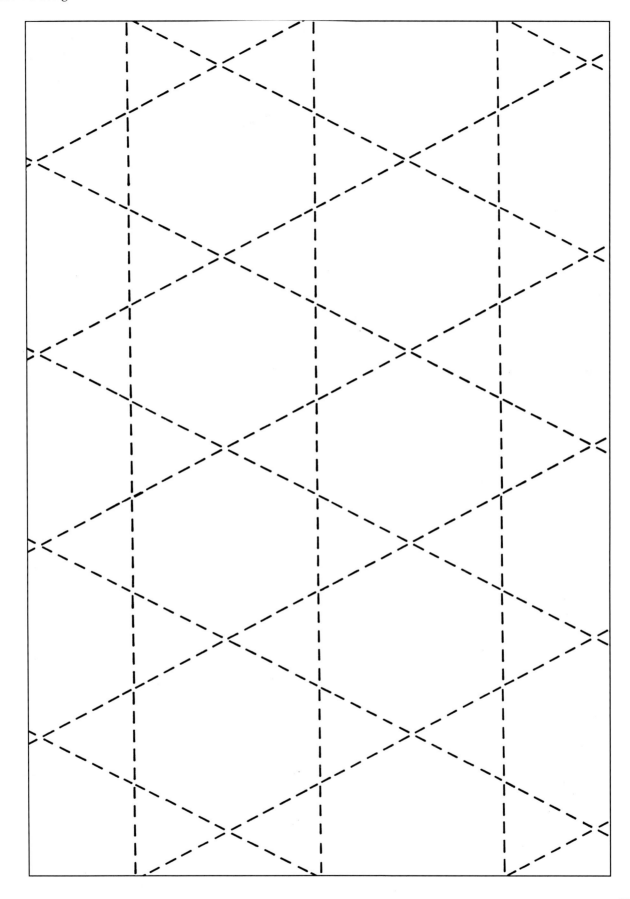

Kikkou (Turtle shell)

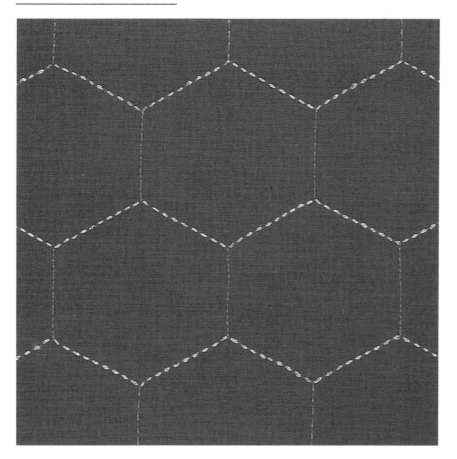

The turtle is an ancient symbol of longevity in Japan. The pattern on its shell is almost perfectly hexagonal.

Designing
Use any size of graph paper. Draw diagonal and vertical lines as shown.

Order of working
Work outwards from the centre of the design. Stitch from *a* to *c* via *b*. Stitch from *c* to *d*, sliding the needle underneath the backing fabric or between the top and the backing fabrics. Then stitch from *d* to *f* via *e*.

Designing

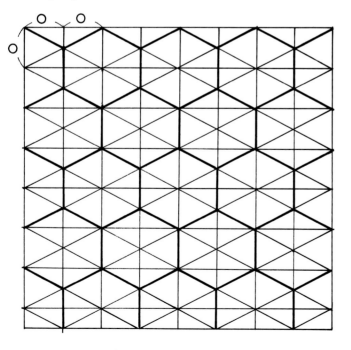

Order of working

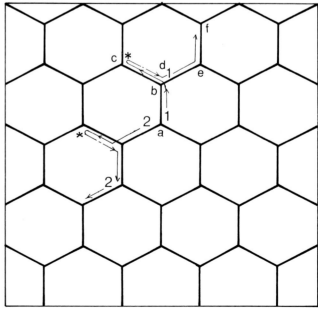

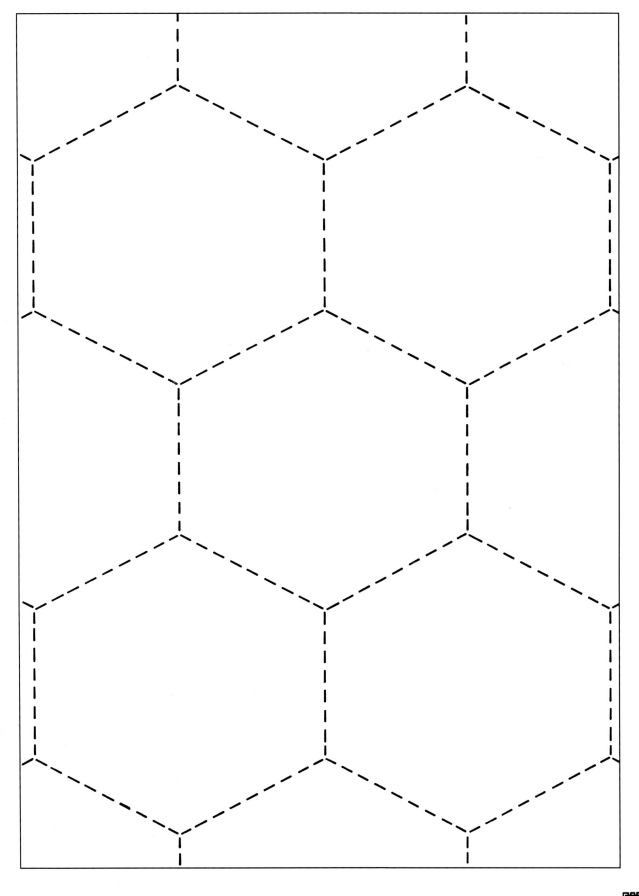

Matsukawa-bishi (Pine-tree bark)

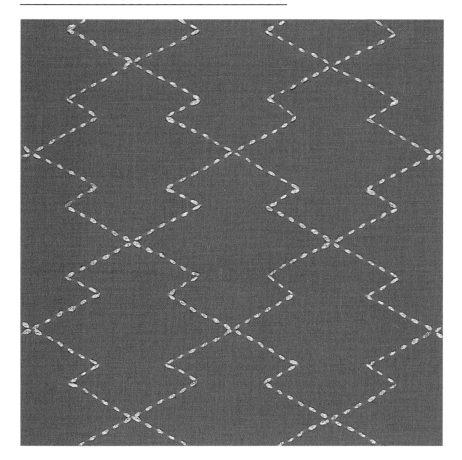

This popular design is used on traditional dress and for the costumes of the Noh theatre, the famous Japanese musical drama with masked actors.

Designing
Use isometric graph paper, or draw diagonal lines on ordinary graph paper.

Order of working
Work outwards from the centre of the design.

Designing   *Order of working*

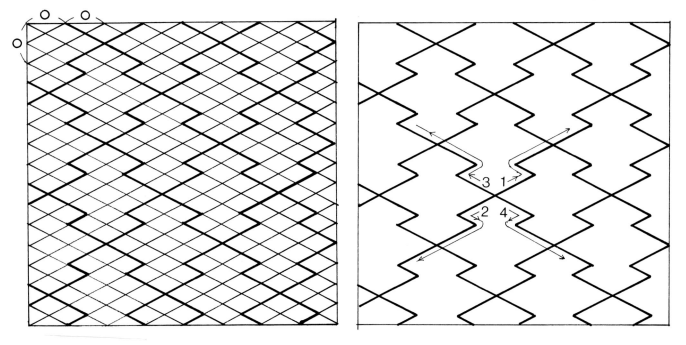

Sayagata (Buddhist symbol)

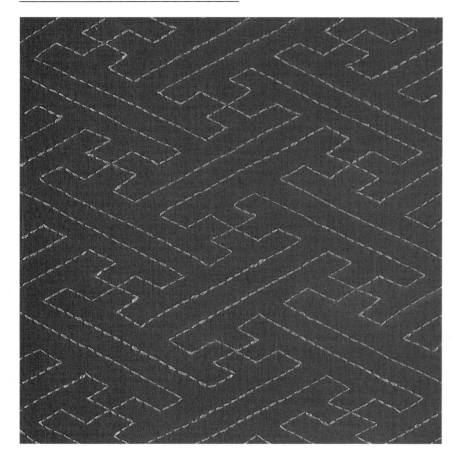

This design came to Japan from India at the same time as Buddhism. The same pattern can be seen on the beams of the Parthenon in Athens.

Designing
Use isometric graph paper, or draw diagonal lines on ordinary graph paper.

Order of working
Work outwards from the centre of the design.

Designing

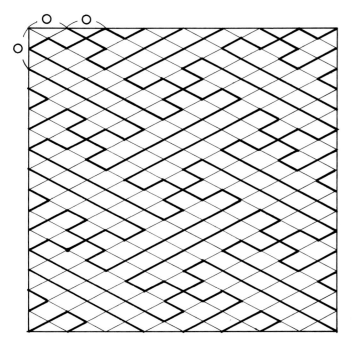

Order of working

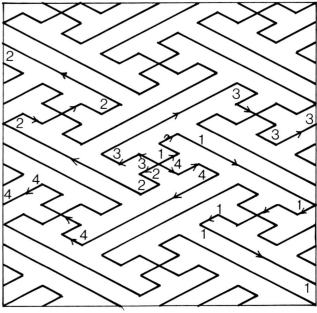

Asa no ha *(Hemp leaf)*

This pattern is traditionally used for babies' clothing. Hemp grows very quickly, and people wish their children to grow like hemp, without illness.

Designing
Draw the diagonal lines as shown, followed by the horizontal and vertical lines.

Order of working
Stitch the vertical lines first, working from the top to the bottom. Stitch the diagonal and then the horizontal lines. Where the stitching line is broken, slide the needle underneath the backing fabric or between the top and backing fabrics.

Designing

Order of working

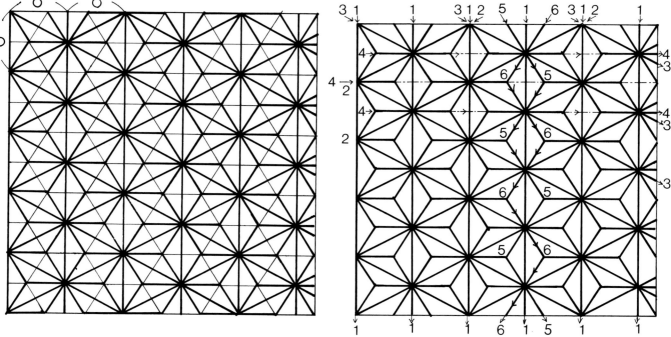

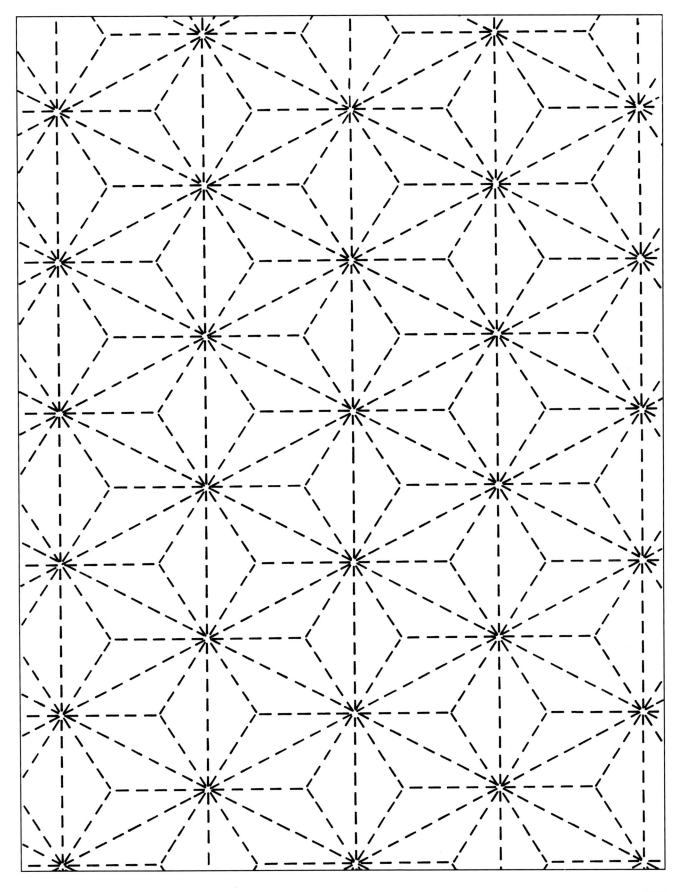

Fundou *(Weight)*

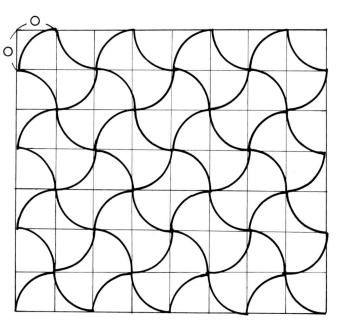

This design comes from the shape of the weight on a set of balance scales.

Designing
Decide the size of circle, then draw a quarter-circle on graph paper.

Order of working
Work outwards from the centre of the design.

Designing

Order of working

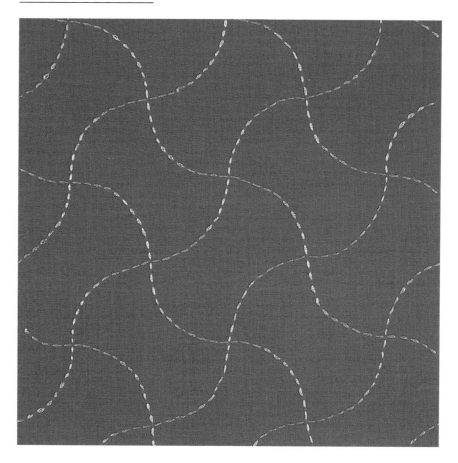

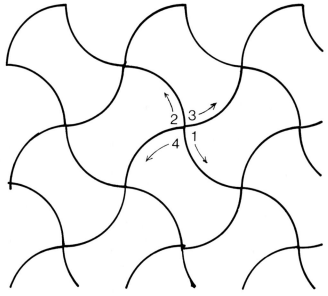

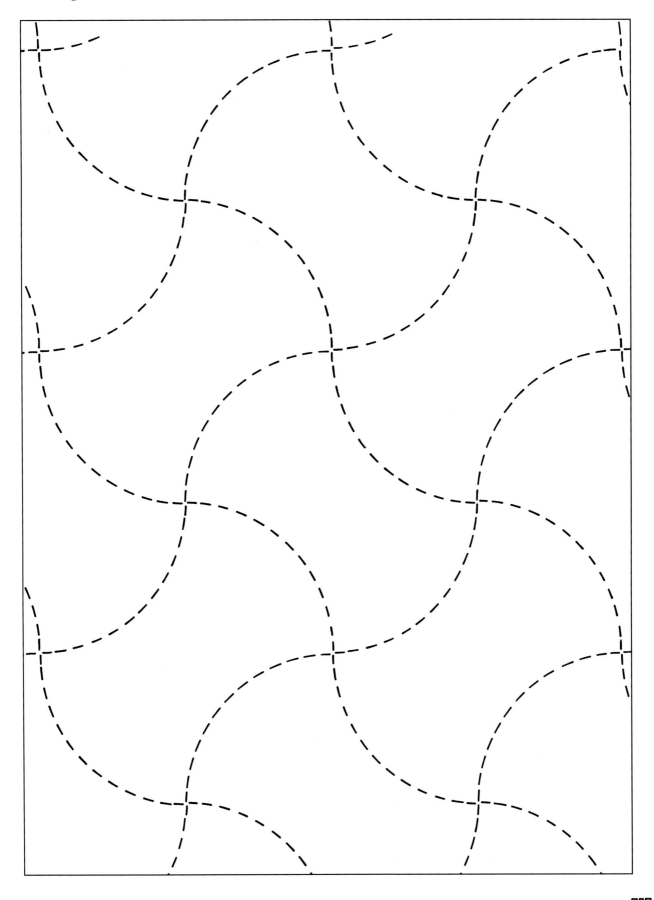

Shippou *(Seven treasures)*

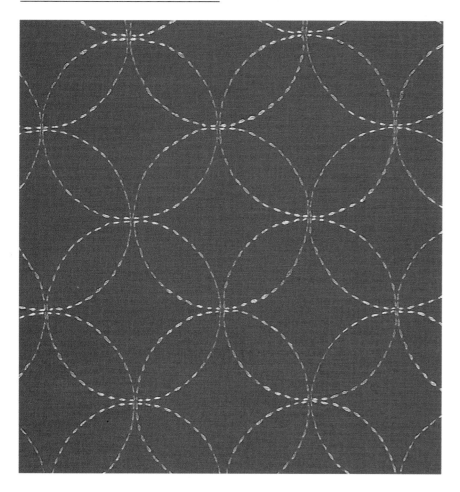

In ancient Asia the seven treasures were gold, silver, lapis lazuli, agate, pearl, coral and crystal.

Designing
Decide the size of circle and draw it on graph paper.

Order of working
Stitch one curved line (1), then turn and stitch in the other direction (2).

Designing

Order of working

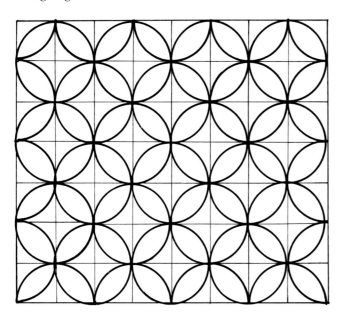

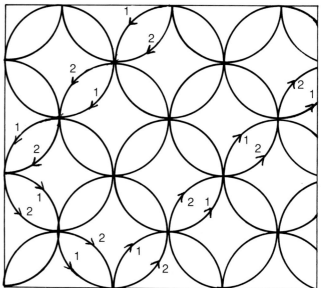

Kaku-shippou (Diamond-shaped seven treasures)

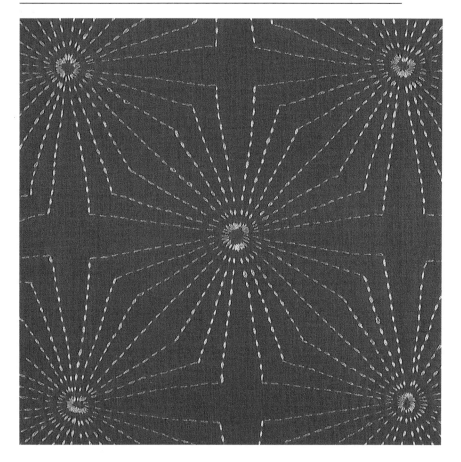

This is a variation of the shippou *pattern, and is used on traditional Japanese garments.*

Designing
Draw a diagonal line on graph paper, as shown.

Order of working
Work the diagonal lines first (1 and 2), then stitch inside the diamond from (3) onwards, as shown.

Designing   *Order of working*

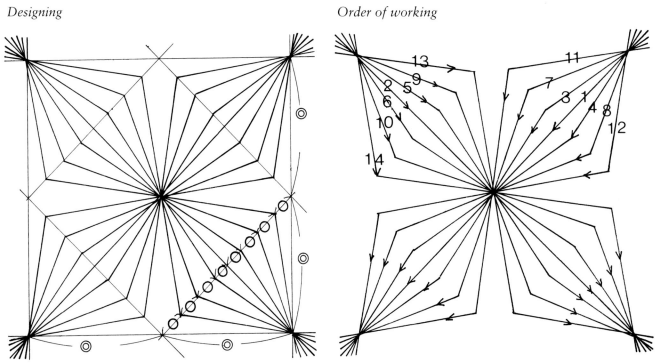

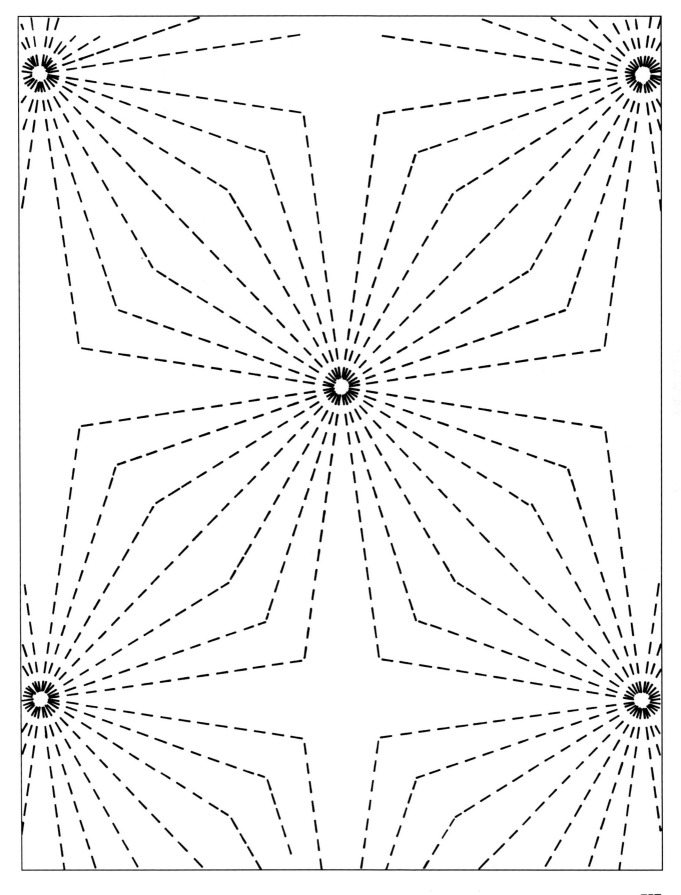

Seigaiha (Waves)

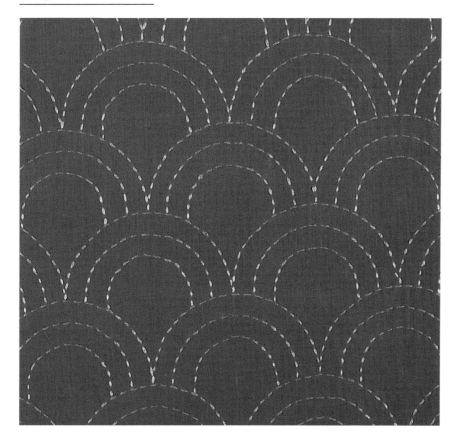

The never-ending motion of the sea is a symbol of eternity and immortality.

Designing
Draw three semi-circles of varying size on graph paper. Extend the straight line of the smallest semi-circle.

Order of working
Work a wave in the order and direction shown. For instructions on how to move from one wave to the next, see fig. 4a and b on page 12.

Designing

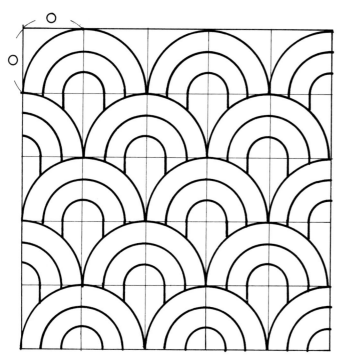

Order of working

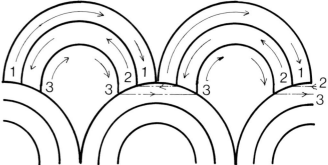

Hishi seigaiha (Diamond-shaped waves)

This pattern is a variation of the seigaiha *design.*

Designing
Using graph paper, draw diagonal lines as shown.

Order of working
Work the diagonal lines first (1 and 2), then stitch inside the diamond (3).

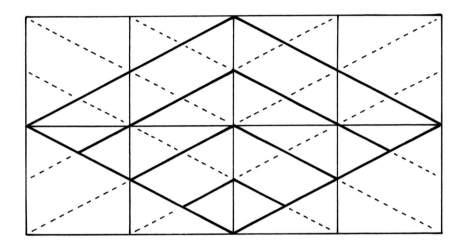

Designing

Order of working

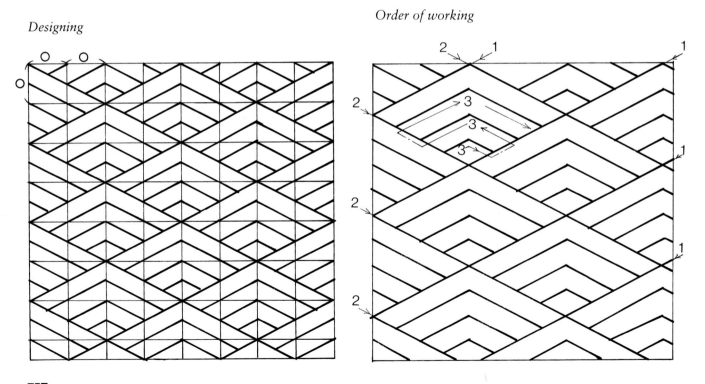

Higaki *(Wooden fence)*

Designing

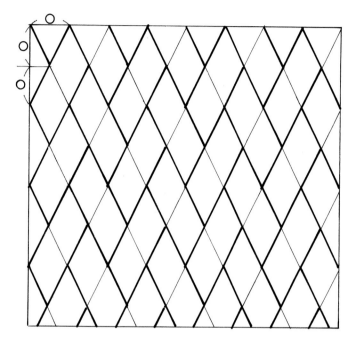

This pattern is inspired by fences made of Japanese cypress.

Designing
Draw diagonal lines on graph paper as shown, then mark alternate lozenges.

Order of working
Stitch along the lines as indicated. Where the stitching line is broken, slide the needle underneath the backing fabric or between the top and backing fabrics (see fig. 4a and b on page 12).

Order of working

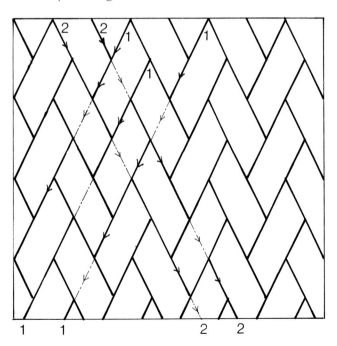

Kiku (*Chrysanthemum*)

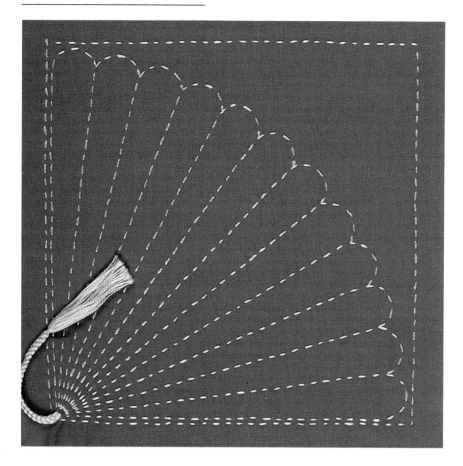

This popular plant was imported from China and has been cultivated in many varieties. In some parts of Japan there are kiku *doll festivals, where the dolls' clothes are covered with chrysanthemum flowers.*

Order of working

Work each petal from the outer edge towards the centre.

Leave long thread ends on each row of stitching, and make a tassel (see pages 125-6).

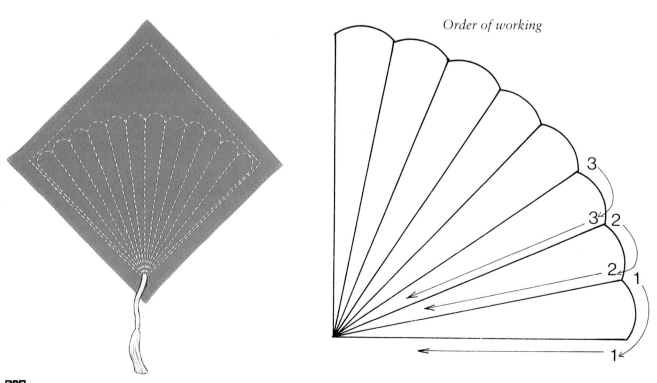

Order of working

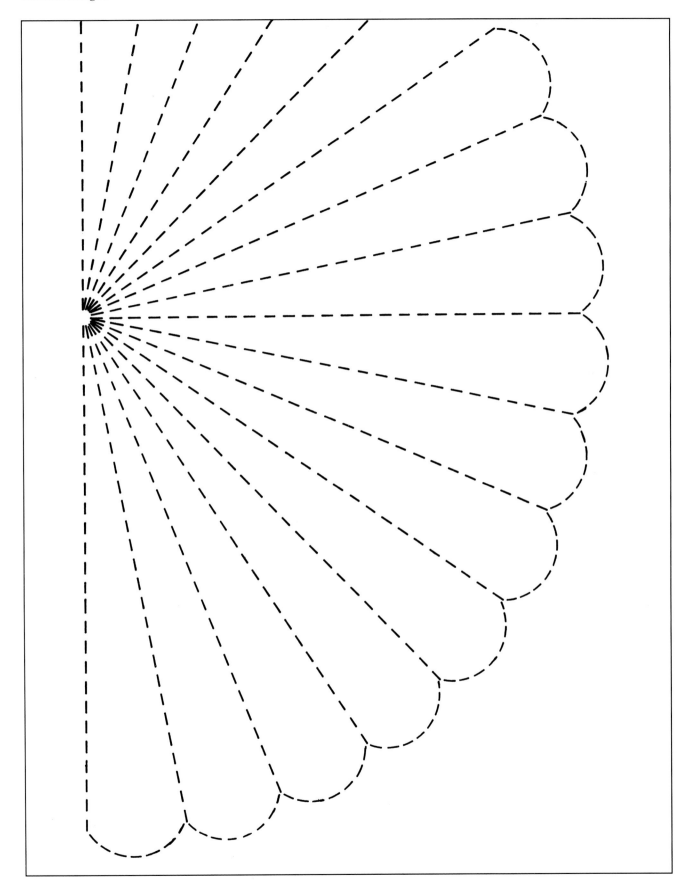

Kiku to karakusa *(Chrysanthemum with scrollwork)*

In Japan the chrysanthemum is a very important flower — the family crest of the Japanese Imperial family.

On 9 September in the Lunar Calendar, the petals of the chrysanthemum are floated on sake, *which is then drunk to give long life. On the previous night, chrysanthemum flowers are covered with cotton, and in the morning the face is wiped with the dew absorbed in the cotton, also to promote long life.*

Designing
Transfer the design to graph paper.

Order of working
Work from the centre of the design outwards, using running stitch and three-stranded cotton.

1 square = 5 cm
(2 in)

Botan (Peony)

The peony is a symbol of nobility and is known in Japan as the Empress of flowers. It is often depicted on kimonos and many other items of daily life.

Designing
Transfer the design to graph paper.

Order of working
Work from the centre of the design outwards, using running stitch and three-stranded cotton.

1 square = 2·5 cm (1 in)
(The design may be worked to any size)

Noshi (Ribbon for tying presents)

This decorative ribbon is used for wrapping presents on ceremonial occasions such as weddings. This design is therefore a symbol of happiness and congratulation.

Designing
Transfer the design to graph paper.

Order of working
Work from the centre of the design outwards, using running stitch and three-stranded cotton.

1 square = 2·5 cm (1 in)
(The design may be worked to any size)

Oshidori (Pair of mandarin ducks)

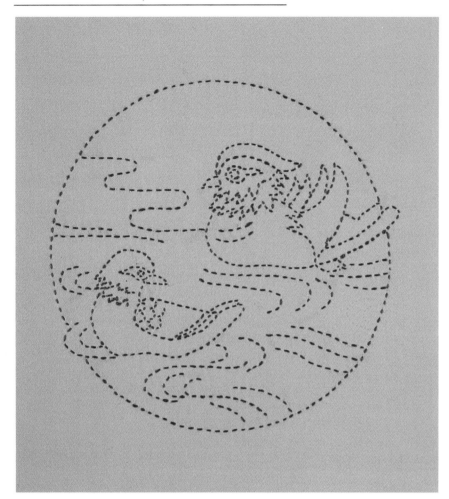

In Japan, mandarin ducks symbolize long-lasting relationships, harmony and prosperity. The Japanese are very fond of this design, and use it for happy occasions.

Designing
Transfer the design to graph paper.

Order of working
Work from the centre of the design outwards, using running stitch and three-stranded cotton.

1 square = 2·5 cm (1 in)
(The design may be worked to any size)

Quilting, appliqué and patchwork designs

This section consists of quilting, appliqué and patchwork designs, which are not made up into finished items as in the next chapter. These designs can be applied to items, garments or accessories of your own choice.

Calico is used as a backing fabric for all the designs. You will need to vary the weight of calico according to the size of the project.

Opposite: **Seigaiha** *(Waves).*

Right: **Tsuru** *(Crane). The method of working this design can be found on page 60.*

Ume (Plum blossom)

1 square = 5 cm (2 in)

You will need
Top fabric: 40 × 50 cm
(15¾ × 19¾ in) brocade
Backing fabric: 40 × 50 cm
(15¾ × 19¾ in) calico
Lining fabric: 40 × 50 cm
(15¾ × 19¾ in)
Appliqué and patchwork fabric
(crêpe de Chine): 10 × 50 cm
(4 × 19¾ in) brown print
(large flower), 10 × 60 cm
(4 × 23½ in) pink print (small
flowers), 10 × 10 cm (4 × 4 in)
red-brown, 10 × 10 cm
(4 × 4 in) pale yellow and
10 × 10 cm (4 × 4 in) pale
pink (buds), 10 × 60 cm
(4 × 23½ in) beige (branch),
10 × 10 cm (4 × 4 in) gold
and 10 × 10 cm (4 × 4 in)
pale green (stamens)
Wadding: 20 × 20 cm
(8 × 8 in), 70 g (2 oz) weight
Anchor stranded cotton: 303

Finished size: 32 × 41 cm
(12½ × 16 in)

Method
Transfer the design to the
relevant appliqué fabrics (see
page 11), allowing a 5 mm (¼ in)
seam all round each shape.

Appliqué the branch on the
background fabric first (see
page 15), then the smaller
flowers and buds, as shown.

Make up the outer petals of
the large central flower in patchwork (see page 16). Cut out the
wadding to the shape of the
completed flower. Appliqué the
flower on top of the branch, as
shown, with the wadding sandwiched underneath. Appliqué
the gold circle in the centre of
the flower.

Embroider French knots on
the top left flower, as shown, to
represent stamens.

Kiri (Paulownia)

1 square = 5 cm (2 in)

You will need

Top fabric: 40 × 50 cm
  (15 ¾ × 19 ¾ in) moss green
Backing fabric: 40 × 50 cm
  (15 ¾ × 19 ¾ in) calico
Lining fabric: 40 × 50 cm
  (15 ¾ × 19 ¾ in)
Reverse-appliqué fabric:
  10 × 40 cm (4 × 15 ¾ in)
  beige, 10 × 40 cm (4 × 15 ¾ in)
  yellow ochre and 10 × 50 cm
  (4 × 19 ¾ in) pale blue (flower
  and leaves), 10 × 10 cm
  (4 × 4 in) mid-blue and
  10 × 20 cm (4 × 8 in)
  maroon (leaf), 10 × 30 cm
  (4 × 11 ¾ in) dark brown
  (branch)
Anchor stranded cotton: 120
  (mid-blue leaf), 167 (pale blue
  leaves), 349 (yellow ochre
  leaves) and 376 (maroon leaf)

Finished size: 32 × 40 cm
  (12 ½ × 15 ¾ in)

Method
Transfer the design to the moss
green top fabric (see page 11).
Work the reverse appliqué in
any order (see page 15-16).
    Embroider the veins of the
leaves in running stitch.

Tsuba (Swordguard)

1 square = 5 cm (2 in)

You will need

Top fabric: 40 × 50 cm
   (15¾ × 19¾ in) olive green
Backing fabric: 40 × 50 cm
   (15¾ × 19¾ in) calico
Reverse-appliqué fabric:
   30 × 40 cm (11¾ × 15¾ in)
   deep blue

Finished size: 32 × 41 cm
   (12½ × 16 in)

Method

Transfer the oval to the pale
green fabric and the design to
the blue fabric (see page 11).

   Place the blue fabric on top of
the pale green fabric and work
the design in reverse appliqué
(see pages 15-16).

Botan (Peony)

1 square = 5 cm (2 in)

You will need
Top fabric: 10 × 70 cm
  (4 × 27½ in) black
Backing fabric: 40 × 90 cm
  (15¾ × 35½ in) calico
Lining fabric: 40 × 50 cm
  (15¾ × 19¾ in)
Patchwork fabric: 10 × 40 cm
  (4 × 15¾ in) sky blue,
  10 × 40 cm (4 × 15¾ in)
  pale blue, 30 × 60 cm
  (11¾ × 23½ in) deep blue
Reverse-appliqué fabric:
  10 × 30 cm (4 × 11¾ in)
  sand, 10 × 30 cm
  (4 × 11¾ in) moss green,
  20 × 20 cm (8 × 8 in)
  orange, 30 × 30 cm
  (11¾ × 11¾ in) yellow ochre

Finished size: 32 × 41 cm
  (12½ × 16 in)

Method
First work the reverse appliqué
(see pages 15-16). Begin with
the orange centre of the large
flower, then work the rest of the
flower followed by the smaller
flowers and leaves.

  Make up the strips and plain-
coloured box shapes in patchwork (see page 16). Appliqué in
position on the peony panels, as
illustrated.

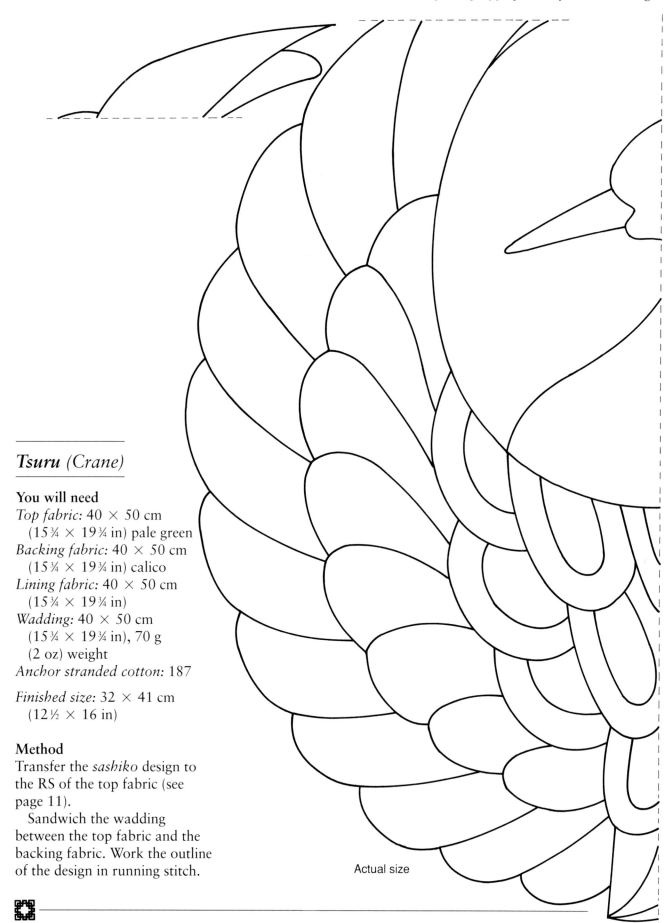

Tsuru (Crane)

You will need
Top fabric: 40 × 50 cm
  (15¾ × 19¾ in) pale green
Backing fabric: 40 × 50 cm
  (15¾ × 19¾ in) calico
Lining fabric: 40 × 50 cm
  (15¾ × 19¾ in)
Wadding: 40 × 50 cm
  (15¾ × 19¾ in), 70 g
  (2 oz) weight
Anchor stranded cotton: 187

Finished size: 32 × 41 cm
  (12½ × 16 in)

Method
Transfer the *sashiko* design to
the RS of the top fabric (see
page 11).
  Sandwich the wadding
between the top fabric and the
backing fabric. Work the outline
of the design in running stitch.

Actual size

Ougi (Fan)

1 square = 5 cm (2 in)

You will need
Top fabric: 40 × 50 cm
  (15¾ × 19¾ in) pale blue
Backing fabric: 40 × 50 cm
  (15¾ × 19¾ in) calico
Lining fabric: 40 × 50 cm
  (15¾ × 19¾ in)
Appliqué fabric: 10 × 20 cm
  (4 × 8 in) blue, 10 × 10 cm
  (4 × 4 in) black and
  20 × 30 cm (8 × 11¾ in)
  yellow ochre (fan),
  10 × 10 cm (4 × 4 in)
  maroon and 10 × 20 cm
  (4 × 8 in) pale green (maple),
  10 × 10 cm (4 × 4 in) pale
  yellow and 10 × 10 cm
  (4 × 4 in) pale pink
  (chrysanthemum),
  10 × 10 cm (4 × 4 in) dark
  green (pine tree), 10 × 10 cm
  (4 × 4 in) grey-green and
  10 × 10 cm (4 × 4 in) pale
  blue-green (leaves),
  20 × 20 cm (8 × 8 in)
  brocade (fan)
Anchor stranded cotton: 23,
  203, 292 (braids), 40 (pink
  chrysanthemum), 307 (yellow
  chrysanthemum and end of
  fan), 216 (leaves), 263 (pine
  tree)

Finished size: 32 × 41 cm
  (12½ × 16 in)

Method
Transfer the appliqué shapes to the relevant fabrics, allowing a 5 mm (¼ in) seam (see page 11). Cut out and appliqué in place (see page 15).

Work the *sashiko* designs on the leaves, the chrysanthemum flowers and the end of the fan in running stitch.

Transfer the 'braids' to the pale blue fabric and backing fabric, on top of the appliqué, where they appear round the edge of the fan. Embroider in stem stitch.

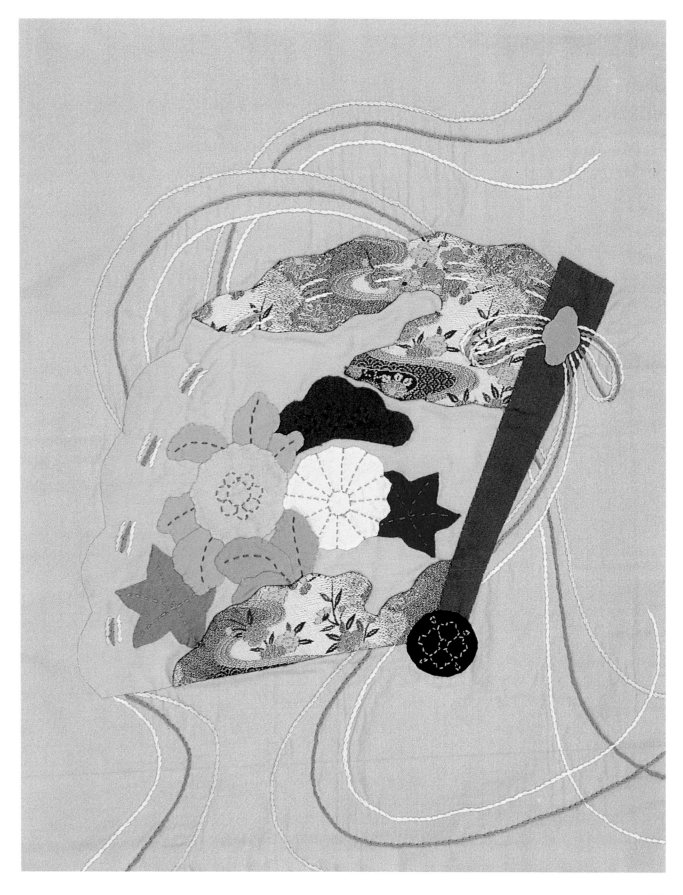

Houou (Phoenix)

1 square = 5 cm (2 in)

'Flame' border: cut eight, four in each of the two patchwork fabrics.

You will need
Top fabric: 60 × 90 cm
   (23½ × 35½ in) small flower
   print
Sashiko fabric: 50 × 50 cm
   (19¾ × 19¾ in) golden brown
Patchwork fabric: 10 × 40 cm
   (4 × 15¾ in) dark red,
   10 × 40 cm (4 × 15¾ in)
   pale blue
Wadding: 50 × 50 cm
   (19¾ × 19¾ in), 70 g (2 oz)
   weight
Anchor stranded cotton: 303

Finished size: 55 × 83 cm
   (21½ × 32½ in)

Method
Transfer the phoenix design to
the RS of the *sashiko* fabric (see
page 11).
   Make a template of the
'flame' border shape, allowing a
5 mm (¼ in) seam all round. Cut
four 'flames' from each of the
two patchwork fabrics and join
to make a circle, alternating the
colours.

Position the 'flame' patchwork
border on top of the *sashiko*
fabric, and appliqué in place
(see page 15). Position the
whole design on the top fabric
and appliqué in place. Sandwich
the wadding between the
sashiko fabric and the backing
fabric. Embroider round the
outline of the design in double
running stitch, stitching through
all three layers.

Ougi (Fan)

You will need

Top fabric: 240 × 90 cm
(94½ × 35½ in) small flower
print

Patchwork fabric: 10 × 40 cm
(4 × 15¾ in) dark red,
10 × 40 cm (4 × 15¾ in)
lilac

Appliqué fabric: 10 × 20 cm
(4 × 8 in) brocade fabric

Anchor stranded cotton: 239,
298

Gold thread

Textile crayons (green, red,
yellow, gold)

Finished size: 75 × 134 cm
(29½ × 52¾ in)

Method

Make a template of an
individual fan segment. Cut out
four shapes from each of the
two patchwork fabrics, allowing
a 5 mm (¼ in) seam all round.
Join the patches together (see
page 16) to make the fan.

Transfer the swirling appliqué
shape to the brocade fabric (see
page 11) and cut out, allowing a
5 mm (¼ in) seam all round.
Position on the edge of the
patchwork fan, as shown, and
appliqué in place (see page 15).

Using the textile crayons,
draw the flowers and leaves.
Embroider round the outlines in
back stitch, using the stranded
cottons. Embroider a line of

running stitch inside the edge of
the brocade shape, as shown.

Position the fan on the top
fabric and appliqué in place.

Cut out an extra shape from
dark red fabric for the base of
the fan, allowing a 5 mm (¼ in)
seam all round. Appliqué in
position, as shown, then
embroider with radiating lines
in running stitch.

Transfer the design for the
gold 'cord' to the top fabric and
embroider in chain stitch, using
the gold thread.

1 square = 5 cm (2 in)

Chou (Butterfly)

1 square = 5 cm (2 in)

You will need

Top fabric: 40 × 50 cm (15¾ × 19¾ in) very pale pink

Backing fabric: 40 × 50 cm (15¾ × 19¾ in) calico

Lining fabric: 40 × 50 cm (15¾ × 19¾ in)

Appliqué fabric (crêpe de Chine): 10 × 10 cm (4 × 4 in) mid-brown (small butterfly wings and large butterfly body), 10 × 20 cm (4 × 8 in) ivory (small and large butterfly wings), 10 × 20 cm (4 × 8 in) dark pink, 10 × 10 cm (4 × 4 in) olive green and 10 × 20 cm (4 × 8 in) mauve (large butterfly wings), 10 × 20 cm (4 × 8 in) print (large butterfly), plus 20 × 40 cm (8 × 15¾ in) blue-patterned brocade (clouds)

Gold thread (antennae)

Anchor stranded cotton: 306 (for couching)

Finished size: 32 × 41 cm (12½ × 16 in)

Method

Transfer the cloud and butterfly shapes to the relevant appliqué fabrics (see page 11). Cut out, allowing a 5 mm (¼ in) seam all round.

Position the shapes on the top fabric and backing fabric, and appliqué in place (see page 15).

Work the butterflies' antennae in couched gold thread.

Ainu

1 square = 5 cm (2 in)

The Ainu people live in the north island of Japan. This is a traditional design for ceremonial garments.

You will need
Top fabric: 40 × 50 cm (15¾ × 19¾ in) black
Backing fabric: 40 × 50 cm (15¾ × 19¾ in) calico
Lining fabric: 40 × 50 cm (15¾ × 19¾ in)
Appliqué fabric: 20 × 60 cm (8 × 23½ in) beige, 20 × 60 cm (8 × 23½ in) dark red, 10 × 40 cm (4 × 15¾ in) moss green, 10 × 50 cm (4 × 19¾ in) sky blue
Anchor stranded cotton: 403, 387

Finished size: 32 × 41 cm (12½ × 16 in)

Method
Transfer the appliqué shapes to the relevant fabrics (see page 11). Cut out, allowing a 5 mm (¼ in) seam all round each shape.

Position the shapes on the top fabric and backing fabric. Appliqué in place (see page 15).

Work the embroidered lines in black chain stitch, and beige running stitch on the dark red shapes.

Matsu (Pine trees)

1 square = 5 cm (2 in)

You will need

Top fabric: 40 × 50 cm
  (15¾ × 19¾ in) yellow
Backing fabric: 40 × 50 cm
  (15¾ × 19¾ in) calico
Lining fabric: 40 × 50 cm
  (15¾ × 19¾ in)
Patchwork fabric: 20 × 40 cm
  (8 × 15¾ in) pale grey,
  10 × 70 cm (4 × 27½ in)
  mushroom
Appliqué fabric: 20 × 30 cm
  (8 × 11¾ in) dark green,
  10 × 70 cm (4 × 27½ in)
  sage green, 20 × 30 cm
  (8 × 11¾ in) emerald green,
  10 × 20 cm (4 × 8 in) dark
  brown, 10 × 20 cm
  (4 × 8 in) red-brown
Gold thread (leaf veins)
Anchor stranded cotton: 306
  (for couching)

Finished size: 32 × 41 cm
  (12½ × 16 in)

Method

First make up the patchwork
triangles (see page 16). Appliqué
these to the yellow background
fabric (see page 15).

Transfer the appliqué shapes
to the relevant fabrics (see
page 11), allowing a 5 mm (¼ in)
seam all round each shape.
Appliqué in position,
overlapping the patchwork as
shown.

Work the veins of the leaves in
couched gold thread.

Suisen *(Narcissus and snowflake)*

1 square = 5 cm (2 in)

You will need

Top fabric: 40 × 50 cm
  (15¾ × 19¾ in) brick red
Backing fabric: 40 × 50 cm
  (15¾ × 19¾ in) calico
Lining fabric: 40 × 50 cm
  (15¾ × 19¾ in)
Appliqué fabric: 10 × 30 cm
  (4 × 11¾ in) pale pink
  (snowflake), 10 × 50 cm
  (4 × 19¾ in) ivory (snowflake), 10 × 20 cm (4 × 8 in)
  pale yellow (flower),
  10 × 10 cm (4 × 4 in) yellow
  (flower), 10 × 20 cm
  (4 × 8 in) pale green (snowflake and leaves), 10 × 30 cm
  (4 × 11¾ in) pale blue-green
  and 10 × 20 cm (4 × 8 in)
  sage green (leaves)
Patchwork fabric: 10 × 30 cm
  (4 × 11¾ in) stone,
  10 × 30 cm (4 × 11¾ in)
  dark brick red
Anchor stranded cotton: 307
  (flower)

Finished size: 32 × 41 cm
  (12½ × 16 in)

Method

Transfer the appliqué shapes to
the relevant fabrics, allowing a
5 mm (¼ in) seam all round each
shape (see page 11). Position on
the top fabric and appliqué in
place (see page 15), overlapping
the flowers and leaves as shown.

  Make up the inner and outer
hexagons in patchwork (see
page 16), to represent a log
cabin. Position over the narcissi
and snowflakes, and appliqué in
place.

  Embroider the narcissi flowers
in double running stitch, as shown.

Genji guruma (Wheel and stream)

You will need
Top fabric: 40 × 50 cm
    (15¾ × 19¾ in) cream
Backing fabric: 40 × 50 cm
    (15¾ × 19¾ in) calico
Lining fabric: 40 × 50 cm
    (15¾ × 19¾ in)
Appliqué fabric: 40 × 50 cm
    (15¾ × 19¾ in) red,
    30 × 30 cm (11¾ × 11¾ in)
    black
Anchor stranded cotton: 20

Finished size: 32 × 41 cm
    (12½ × 16 in)

Method
Transfer the relevant shapes to
the red appliqué fabric (see
page 11), allowing a 5 mm (¼ in)
seam all round each shape, and
cut out. Position on the top
fabric and the backing fabric,
and appliqué in place (see page
15).

Appliqué the black wheel on
to the red fabric.

Embroider lines to indicate
the flowing water in the stream
in double running stitch.

1 square = 5 cm (2 in)

Tessen (Clematis)

1 square = 5 cm (2 in)

You will need
*Patchwork and appliqué
    fabric:* 20 × 40 cm
    (8 × 15¾ in) dark red,
    20 × 40 cm (8 × 15¾ in)
    dark green, 20 × 40 cm
    (8 × 15¾ in) beige,
    10 × 60 cm (4 × 23½ in)
    pale blue (flower and tendril),
    10 × 40 cm (4 × 15¾ in)
    dark brown (flower),
    10 × 40 cm (4 × 15¾ in)
    pale green (leaves),
    10 × 20 cm (4 × 8 in) white
    (leaves)
Backing fabric: 40 × 50 cm
    (15¾ × 19¾ in) calico
Lining fabric: 40 × 50 cm
    (15¾ × 19¾ in)
Anchor stranded cotton: 261
    (pale blue flower), 269 (pale
    green leaves), 843 (white
    leaf), 880 (dark brown
    flower)

Finished size: 32 × 41 cm
    (12½ × 16 in)

Method
Cut out two rectangles from
each of the patchwork fabrics.
Place the rectangles RS together,
stitch and press flat.

Transfer the appliqué shapes
to the relevant fabrics (see
page 11), allowing a 5 mm (¼ in)
seam all round each shape. Cut
out and position on the
patchwork as shown. Appliqué
in place (see page 15).

Embroider the flowers and
leaves in running stitch and
double running stitch.

Tsuru no watari (Cranes of passage)

1 square = 5 cm (2 in)

You will need

Appliqué fabric: 30 × 40 cm
   (11¾ × 15¾ in) pale
   turquoise, 40 cm × 1·4 m
   (15¾ × 55 in) mauve,
   20 × 40 cm (8 × 15¾ in)
   pale pink
Patchwork fabric: 10 × 30 cm
   (4 × 11¾ in) grey-green,
   10 × 10 cm (4 × 4 in)
   maroon, 10 × 20 cm
   (4 × 8 in) pale yellow,
   10 × 30 cm (4 × 11¾ in)
   beige, 10 × 10 cm (4 × 4 in)
   pale blue, 10 × 10 cm
   (4 × 4 in) of two different
   brocade prints
*Patchwork and appliqué
   fabric:* 10 × 40 cm
   (4 × 15¾ in) crêpe de Chine
   print
Backing fabric: 40 x 50 cm
   (15¾ × 19¾ in) calico
Gold thread (cranes)
Anchor stranded cotton: 306
(for couching)

Finished size: 32 × 41 cm
   (12½ × 16 in)

Method

Transfer the appliqué shapes
to the relevant fabrics (see
page 11), allowing a 5 mm (¼ in)
seam, and cut out. Lay on the
backing fabric and appliqué in
position (see page 15).

   Make templates of the
hexagonal patchwork shapes
(see overleaf). Cut out in the
relevant fabrics, allowing a
5 mm (¼ in) seam all round.
Make up the two areas of
patchwork as shown (see
page 16). Appliqué in position
on the appliqué background.

   Transfer the images of the
flying cranes and work in
couched gold thread, using the
thread double.

*Couching the cranes: follow the
direction of the arrows for the
order of stitching.*

Actual size

1 square = 1 cm (⅜ in)

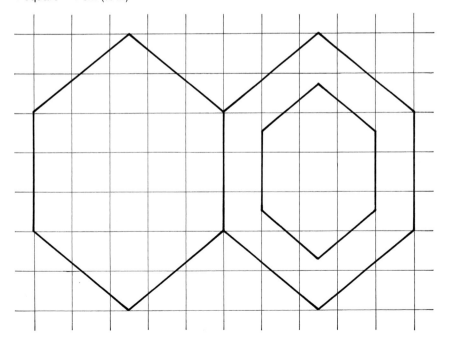

5

Projects

In most of the following projects, calico is used as a backing fabric.
The weight of calico varies according to the size of the project.

Placemat

Seigaiha (Waves)

This is a variation of the wave
design shown on pages 34-5.

You will need
Top fabric: 40 × 50 cm
   (15¾ × 19¾ in) mid-blue
Backing fabric: 40 × 50 cm
   (15¾ × 19¾ in) calico
Lining fabric: 40 × 50 cm
   (15¾ × 19¾ in)
Anchor stranded cotton: 855

Finished size of placemat:
   45 × 33 cm (17¾ × 13 in)

1 square = 5 cm (2 in)

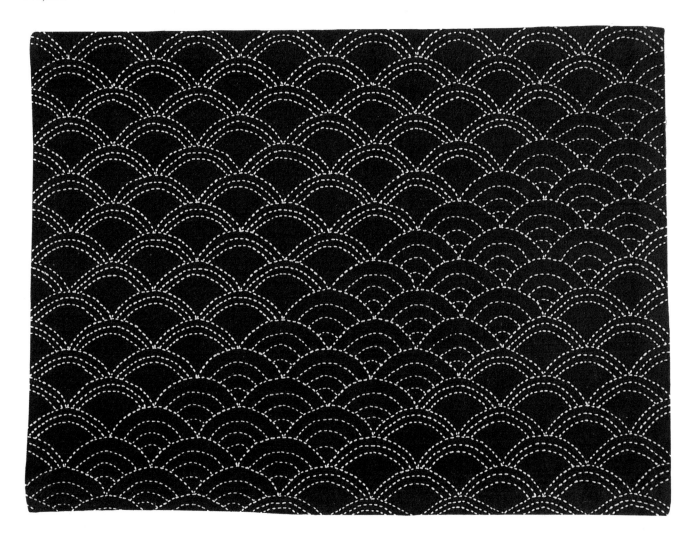

Method
Transfer the design to the top fabric (see page 11). Place the top fabric and backing fabric WS together on a flat surface. Pin, tack and then stitch the two fabrics together, using running stitch.

Place these two fabrics and the lining fabric RS together. With a 1 cm (⅜ in) seam allowance, stitch round three sides, leaving one short side open. Turn RS out and oversew the fourth side.

Placemat

Sakura (Cherry blossom)

You will need

Top fabric: 30 × 40 cm
  (11¾ × 15¾ in) pale blue-green
Backing fabric: 30 × 40 cm
  (11¾ × 15¾ in) calico
Appliqué fabric: 20 × 30 cm
  (8 × 11¾ in) darker blue-green
Wadding: 30 × 40 cm
  (11¾ × 15¾ in), 70 g (2 oz)
  weight
Anchor stranded cotton: 368
  (flowers), 266 (leaves and
  branches), 214 (clouds)
Finished size of placemat:
  30 × 22 cm (12 × 8½ in)

Method

Transfer the cherry-blossom design to the top fabric (see page 11). Cut out the cloud shape from the appliqué fabric, leaving a 5 mm (¼ in) seam, and appliqué to the top fabric (see page 15).

Place the backing fabric, wadding and top fabric together, with the wadding sandwiched in the middle and the RS of the top fabric uppermost. Pin and tack through all three fabrics, then embroider the design in running stitch, with chain stitch for the branch and French knots for the stems. Stitch the lines on the cloud in running stitch, using three threads for the upper line and one thread for the lower line.

Cut the wadding to the finished size. Turn under a 1 cm (⅜ in) seam on both the top fabric and the backing fabric, then stitch the two fabrics together with running stitches 2-3 mm (⅛ in) from the edge.

Actual size

Tea cosy

Fuji to hanabishi (Wistaria and diamond-shaped flower)

You will need

Top fabric: 40 × 90 cm
    (15¾ × 35½ in) pale purple
Backing fabric: 40 × 90 cm
    (15¾ × 35½ in) calico
Wadding: 40 × 90 cm
    (15¾ × 35½ in), 70 g (2 oz)
    weight
60 cm (23½ in) cord
Anchor stranded cotton: 112

Finished size of tea cosy:
    35 × 29 cm (13¾ × 11½ in)

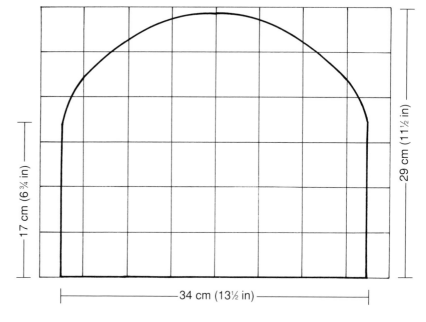

17 cm (6¾ in)

29 cm (11½ in)

34 cm (13½ in)

Method

Fold the top fabric in half and draw a curved line for the shape of the tea cosy, as shown. Cut out, then cut the fabric in half to give two tea-cosy shapes. Do the same for the backing fabric and the wadding.

Transfer the design to one piece of top fabric (see page 11). Place each piece of top fabric and lining fabric RS together, with the wadding sandwiched in between.

Leaving a 1 cm (⅜ in) seam allowance, stitch round the curved edge, leaving the straight sides open. Turn RS out and embroider the *sashiko* design in running stitch.

Place the two halves of the tea cosy RS together. Stitch round the curved edge, leaving a 1 cm (⅜ in) seam. Clip the seam and turn RS out. To finish the straight bottom edge, fold the top and backing fabric to the inside. Hand stitch in running stitch 2-3 mm (¹⁄₁₆ in) from the edge.

Make a tassel and knot it decoratively (see pages 125–6 and 119–20) and stitch in place in the centre top, as illustrated.

Actual size

Cushion

Sakura (Cherry blossom)

You will need

Patchwork fabric: 30 × 90 cm
(11¾ × 35½ in) golden
yellow, 30 × 90 cm
(11¾ × 35½ in) moss green

Backing fabric: 50 × 90 cm
(19¾ × 35½ in) calico

Appliqué fabric: 10 × 20 cm
(4 × 8 in) pink, 10 × 20 cm
(4 × 8 in) dark red and
10 × 40 cm (4 × 15¾ in)
red-brown (flowers),
10 × 50 cm (4 × 19¾ in)
pale green (leaves),
10 × 20 cm (4 × 8 in) pale
brown (stem)

Anchor stranded cotton: 845
(leaf veins), 337 (stamens)

35 cm (13¾ in) zip fastener

Finished size of cushion:
42 × 42 cm (16½ × 16½ in)

Method

Work the patchwork first (see
page 16). Make a template,
using the shape below, then join

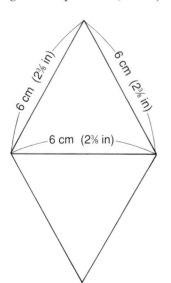

enough patches to make a
square slightly larger than the
finished cushion size.

Transfer the design to the
appliqué fabrics (see page 11)
and cut out, leaving a 5 mm
(¼ in) seam round each shape.
Appliqué on top of the RS of
the patchwork (see page 15).
Embroider the stamens of the

flower in French knots and the
veins on the leaves in double
running stitch.

Place the cushion cover and
the backing fabric RS together.
Stitch along three sides, and
3·5 cm (1½ in) at either end of
the fourth side. Turn RS out.
Insert the zip fastener in the
opening and stitch in position.

1 square =
5 cm (2 in)

Cushion

Ume (Plum blossom)

You will need

Top fabric: 50 × 90 cm
   (19¾ × 35½ in) black
   (cushion), 30 × 90 cm
   (11¾ × 35½ in) pale yellow
   (buttercup)
Backing fabric: 50 × 90 cm
   (19¾ × 35½ in) calico
Lining fabric: 50 × 90 cm
   (19¾ × 35½ in)
Reverse-appliqué fabric:
   40 × 40 cm (15¾ × 15¾ in)
   red-brown
Appliqué fabric: 10 × 20 cm
   (4 × 8 in) pale pink and
   10 × 10 cm (4 × 4 in) pink
   (flowers), 10 × 40 cm (4 ×
   15¾ in) brown (branch), 10 ×
   10 cm (4 × 4 in) light green
Wadding: 30 × 30 cm
   (11¾ × 11¾ in), 70 g (2 oz)
   weight
Anchor stranded cotton: 347
   (family crest), 303 (stamens)
Gold thread (stamens)
35 cm (13¾ in) zip fastener

Finished size of cushion:
   42 × 42 cm (16½ × 16½ in)

Method
Transfer the blossom design to
the appliqué fabrics (see page 11),
allowing a 5 mm (¼ in) seam
round each shape, and cut out.

   Cut a circle out of the yellow
fabric, following the outer
cutting line. Position the branch
and blossom on it as shown,
and appliqué in place (see
page 15). Cut the same-sized
circle out of the red-brown
reverse-appliqué fabric. Place
the wadding and backing fabric

behind the appliqué circle, then
stitch over the design outline.

   Embroider the three family-
crest motifs in running stitch.
Work the stamens in couched
gold thread and French knots.

   Reverse appliqué the yellow
circle in the centre of the black
fabric (see pages 15-16), with

the red-brown circle sandwiched
in between.

   Place the cushion cover and
the backing fabric RS together.
Stitch along three sides, and
3·5 cm (1½ in) at either end of
the fourth side. Turn RS out.
Insert the zip fastener and stitch
in place.

1 square =
5 cm (2 in)

Drawstring bag

Matsu-take-nami (Pine tree, bamboo leaves and waves)

You will need

Top fabric: 40 × 90 cm
(15¾ × 35½ in) pale green
Lining fabric: 40 × 110 cm
(15¾ × 43 in) pale green
Patchwork fabric: 10 × 30 cm
(4 × 11¾ in) each of pale
blue-green, pale brown and
pale blue, 10 × 60 cm
(4 × 23½ in) each of flower
print and mid-brown
Stiffening: 20 × 20 cm
(8 × 8 in) Vilene
Anchor stranded cotton: 800
(waves), 266 (bamboo), 268
(pine tree)
2 m (79 in) cord
Eight 16 mm (½ in) curtain rings
Finished size of bag: 18 cm (7 in)
deep × 17 cm (6¾ in) diameter

Method

Work the patchwork first. Trace
the hexagon shape and make a
template. Cut an equal number
of patches from the different
patchwork fabrics, leaving a
5 mm (¼ in) seam allowance.

Transfer the *sashiko* designs
to the fabric hexagons (see
page 11) and embroider. Use
running stitch for the waves,
and running and double running
stitch for the bamboo and pine
tree. Join the patches in two
long strips, alternating the fabrics.

Make a template for the
zigzag band round the centre of
the patchwork. Cut out from
the mid-brown fabric, leaving a

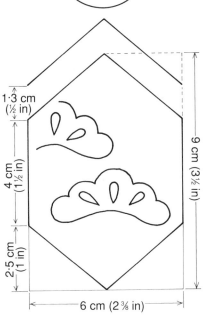

17 cm
(6¾ in)
Gusset

1·3 cm
(½ in)

4 cm
(1½ in)

2·5 cm
(1 in)

9 cm (3½ in)

6 cm (2⅜ in)

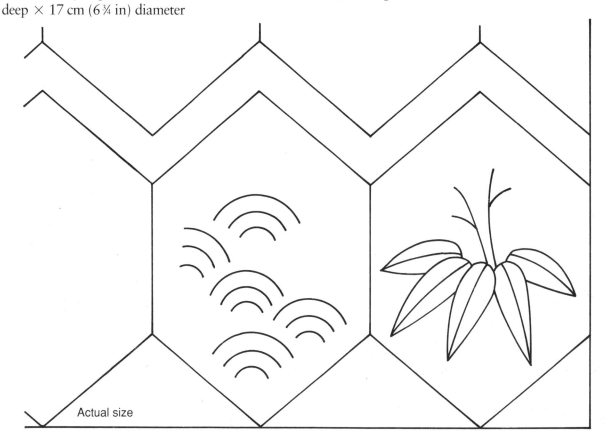

Actual size

5 mm (¼ in) seam allowance on either side. Position between the two rows of patchwork, following the hexagon angles, and hem.

Cut out an 18 × 54 cm (7 × 21 in) rectangle from the top fabric. Centre the patchwork face up on the RS. Hem the top and bottom edges of the patchwork. Place the two short ends of the rectangle RS together, and stitch, leaving a 1 cm (⅜ in) seam allowance.

Cut a rectangle 18 × 54 cm (7 × 21 in) from the lining material, and two 17 cm (6¾ in) diameter circles from the lining material and one from the Vilene for the base. Stitch the short ends of the lining as above, then place the lining inside the patchwork bag, WS together. With the Vilene sandwiched in between the two fabric circles, place the base in position. Machine stitch the bag to the base, then turn in the top edges of the bag and stitch.

Attach the curtain rings at regular intervals round the top of the bag. Cut the cord into two equal lengths, thread through the rings and knot decoratively (see pages 119-20).

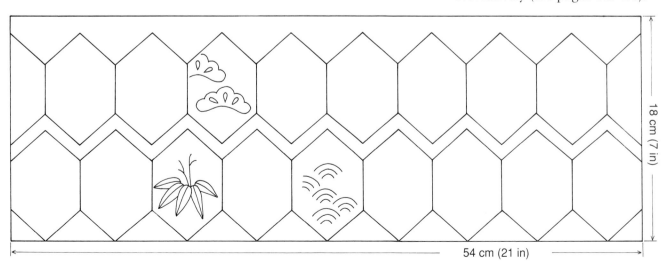

Teddy bear's jacket

Igeta (Square patterns)

You will need

Top fabric: 30 × 60 cm
  (11¾ × 23½ in) dark blue
Lining fabric: 30 × 60 cm
  (11¾ × 23½ in)
Sashiko thread (see page 9):
  white *or* off-white
Anchor thread: coton à broder
  387 *or* stranded cotton 387

Finished size of jacket: 26 cm
  (10 in) wide × 22 cm (8½ in)

Method

Cut out the pattern pieces,
following the cutting layout,
and label *a*, *b*, *c*, *d*, *e*, *f*. Transfer
the *sashiko* design to the top
fabric (see page 11). Embroider
in running stitch.

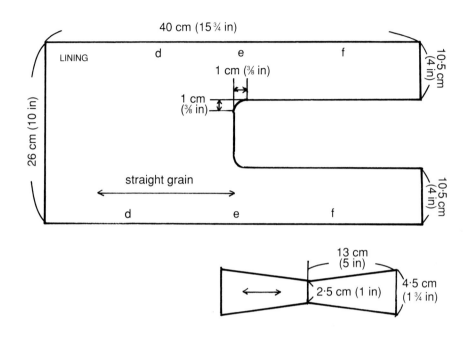

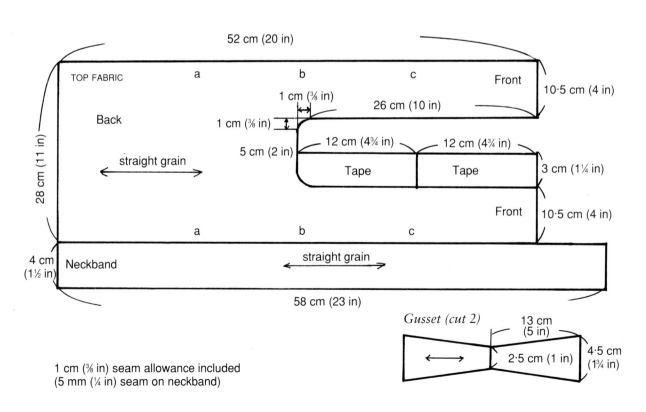

1 cm (⅜ in) seam allowance included
(5 mm (¼ in) seam on neckband)

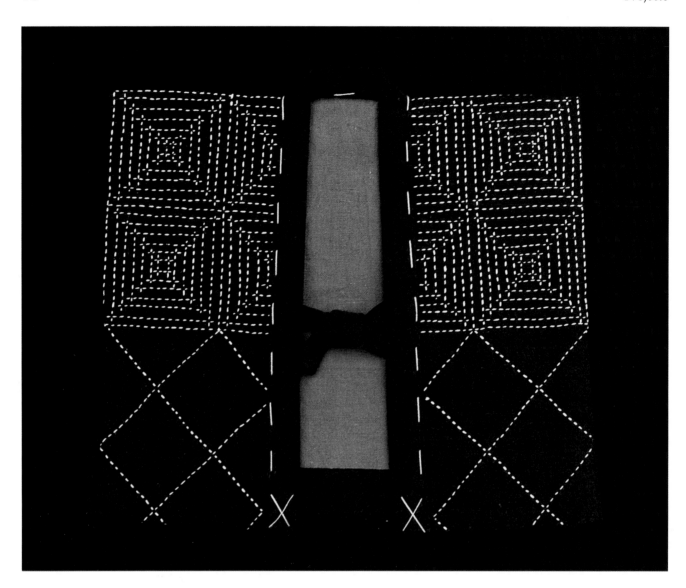

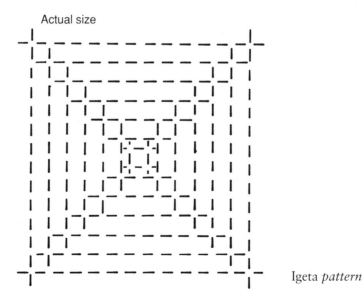

Actual size

Igeta *pattern*

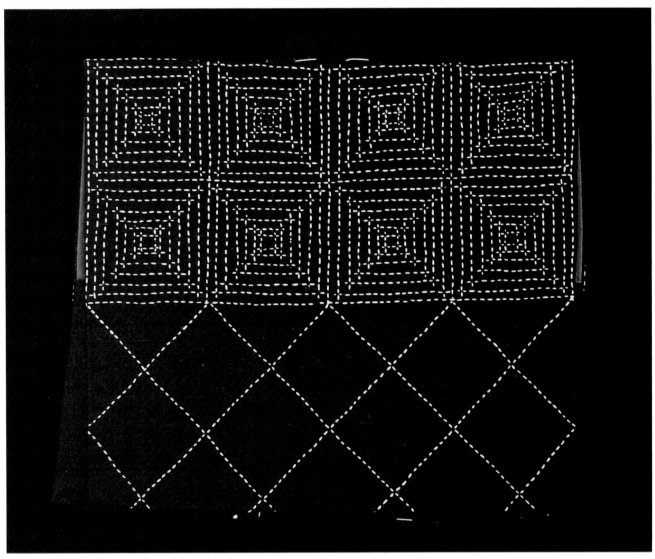

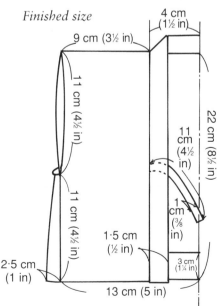

Finished size

4 cm (1½ in)

9 cm (3½ in)

11 cm (4½ in)

22 cm (8½ in)

11 cm (4½ in)

11 cm (4½ in)

1 cm (⅜ in)

2·5 cm (1 in)

1·5 cm (½ in)

3 cm (1¼ in)

13 cm (5 in)

Lay the top fabric on a flat surface and place the lining on top, RS together. Pin *a* to *d*, *b* to *e* and *c* to *f*. Machine stitch both side seams from *a* to *c*.

Turn under a 3 cm (1¼ in) seam allowance on the bottom of the top fabric and the lining, on both front and back, and stitch. Turn the jacket inside out.

Fold each gusset in half, RS inside, and stitch across the top (narrow) part. Turn RS out. Slide one gusset between the top and lining fabric on one side of the jacket, and stitch to the back and front, leaving a 1 cm (⅜ in) seam allowance. Repeat with the other gusset.

Stitch the neckband to the jacket top, leaving a 5 mm (¼ in) seam allowance. Turn the neckband to the RS of the jacket front and stitch again. Fold the neckband 1·5 cm (½ in) from the stitching line, then fold again 3 cm (1¼ in) further, and stitch with herringbone stitch. Fold under each end of the neckband seam and stitch.

Make two tapes 11 cm (4½ in) long and 1 cm (⅜ in) wide and stitch in place on either side of the jacket.

Apron

Namima no chidori (Plover flying over waves)

You will need

Apron fabric: 60 × 90 cm
  (23½ × 35½ in)
Appliqué fabric: 50 × 60 cm
  (19¾ × 23½ in) pale blue
  (waves), 20 × 20 cm
  (8 × 8 in) very pale blue-
  green (plover)
Anchor stranded cotton: 131
  (eye), 158 (claw, beak and
  bubbles)
Bias binding: 90 cm (35½ in)
Tape: 1·4 m (55 in) × 1·5 cm
  (½ in) wide

Finished size of apron:
  50 × 75 cm (19¾ × 29½ in)

Method

Cut out the apron shape, adding
a seam allowance of 3 cm (1¼ in)
either side and 5 mm (¼ in) top
and bottom.

Transfer the waves and plover
design to the appliqué fabrics
(see page 11), allowing a 5 mm
(¼ in) seam all round. Appliqué
on the RS of the apron fabric
(see page 15).

Work the surface embroidery
in chain stitch, filling in the
bird's eye with stitches.

Fold under half the seam
allowance on either side of the
apron, fold again, press and
machine stitch. Repeat for the
top and bottom edges.

With RS together, machine
stitch the bias binding round the
armholes and top edge of the
apron. Fold the binding over to
the WS and machine stitch to
secure. Cut the tape into two
lengths 40 cm (15¾ in) long, one

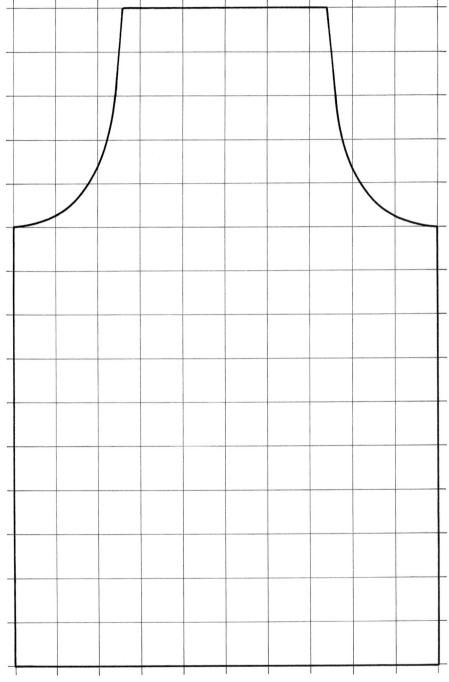

1 square = 5 cm (2 in)

for each side of the apron, and
one length 60 cm (23½ in) long,

to go round the neck. Stitch in
place.

1 square = 5 cm
(2 in)

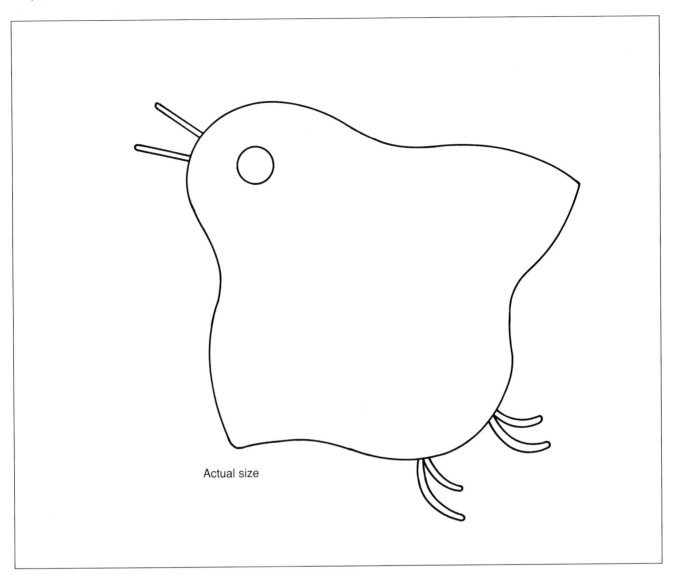

Actual size

Waistcoat

Sodenash (Bamboo leaf and feathered arrow)

You will need

Top fabric: 1·3 m × 90 cm
(51 × 35½ in)

Lining fabric: 1·3 m × 90 cm
(51 × 35½ in)

Appliqué fabric: 10 × 40 cm
(4 × 15¾ in) blue-green
(bamboo leaves)

*Patchwork and reverse-appliqué
fabric:* 10 × 30 cm
(4 × 11¾ in) pale blue,
10 × 30 cm (4 × 11¾ in)
purple

Wadding: 20 × 40 cm
(8 × 15¾ in), 70 g (2 oz)
weight

Anchor stranded cotton: 303
2 m (78¾ in) cord

Finished size of waistcoat:
54 cm (21¼ in) wide × 62 cm
(24½ in)

Method

Transfer the bamboo-leaf shapes
to the appliqué fabric (see
page 11). Cut each leaf out
separately, allowing a 5 mm
(¼ in) seam all round, then join
them together as illustrated. Cut
out the shape of each bunch of
leaves in wadding.

Cut out the waistcoat shape
in the top fabric and also in
lining fabric. Appliqué the
bamboo leaves in position on
the RS of the waistcoat fronts
(see page 15), as shown
overleaf, with the wadding
sandwiched in between.
Embroider the leaf veins and
branches in running stitch.

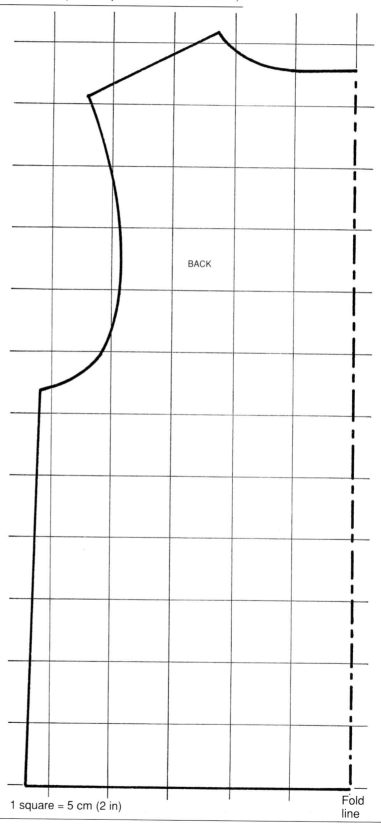

BACK

1 square = 5 cm (2 in)

Fold
line

With RS together, join the
waistcoat fronts to the back,
leaving a 1 cm (⅜ in) seam.
Repeat for the lining. Place the
waistcoat and lining RS together
and stitch, leaving the bottom
edge open. Clip the underarm
curve and turn RS out. Stitch
the bottom edge.

Trace the templates for the
patchwork design (see page 16),
allowing an 8 mm (⅜ in) seam
all round. Make up the two
pieces of patchwork (see page 16).

Set the patchwork into the
waistcoat fronts, using the
reverse-appliqué technique (see
pages 15-16).

Make a butterfly button and
buttonhole (see pages 121-4)
and stitch in position on the
waistcoat fronts, as shown in
the photograph on the previous
page.

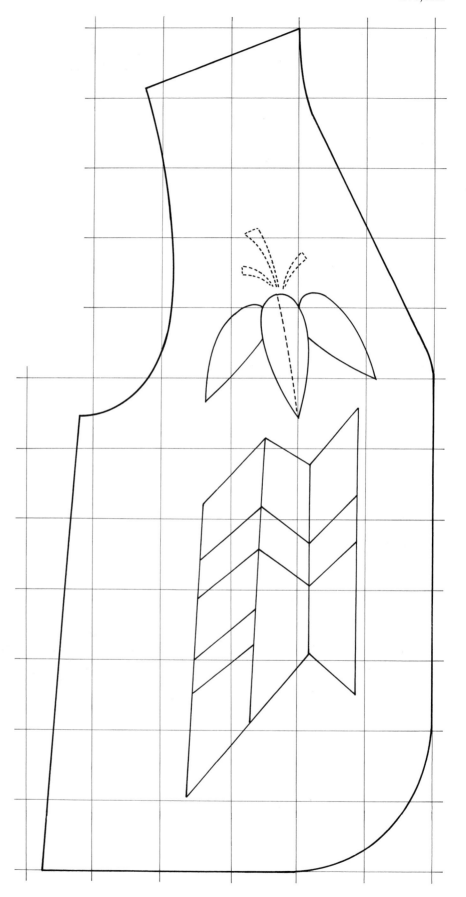

1 square = 5 cm (2 in)

(NB Seam allowances not included)

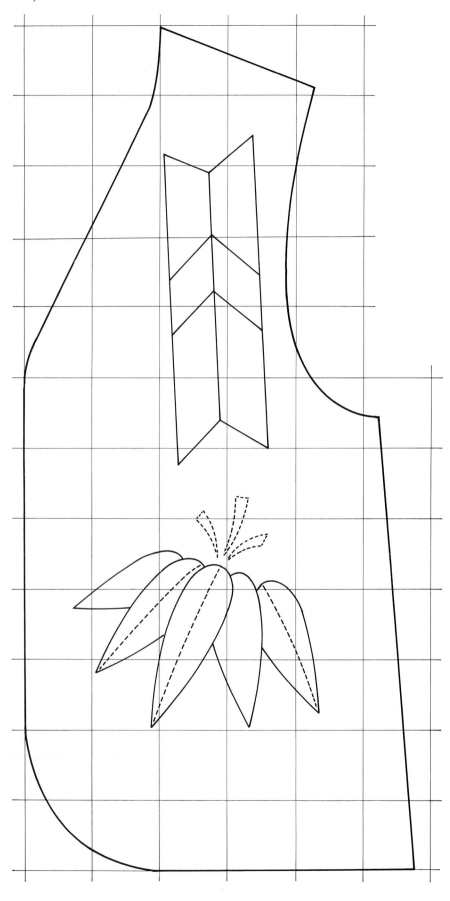

Wallhanging

Tsuru to kame (Crane and turtle)

You will need

Top fabric: 80 × 80 cm
(31½ × 31½ in) indigo blue
Backing fabric: 80 × 80 cm
(31½ × 31½ in) calico
Lining fabric: 80 × 80 cm
(31½ × 31½ in)
Reverse-appliqué fabric:
50 × 50 cm (19¾ × 19¾ in)
off-white, 40 × 40 cm
(15¾ × 15¾ in) striped
Appliqué fabric: 50 × 50 cm
(19¾ × 19¾ in) pale blue
Anchor stranded cotton: 926

Finished size of wallhanging:
76 × 76 cm (30 × 30 in)

Method

(See chart overleaf)
Transfer the circle to the RS of
the top fabric (see page 11). Lay
the off-white fabric underneath.
Cut the same-sized circle in the
pale blue fabric, allowing a
5 mm (¼ in) seam, and appliqué
in position (see page 15).

Cut the crane and turtle out
of the striped fabric, allowing a
5 mm (¼ in) seam, and position
on the off-white fabric. Work
the design in reverse appliqué
(see pages 15-16), and
embroider in chain stitch.

Lay the top fabric on a flat
surface with the lining on top,
RS together, and pin together.
With a 1 cm (⅜ in) seam
allowance, machine stitch round
all four sides, leaving a 20 cm
(8 in) gap open in the centre of
one side. Fold the seam
allowances on two opposite
sides of the wallhanging in over
the lining, 2 mm (⅟₁₆ in) inside
the sewing line, and herringbone
stitch. Repeat for the seam
allowances on the remaining
two sides. Turn the wallhanging
inside out and oversew the
opening.

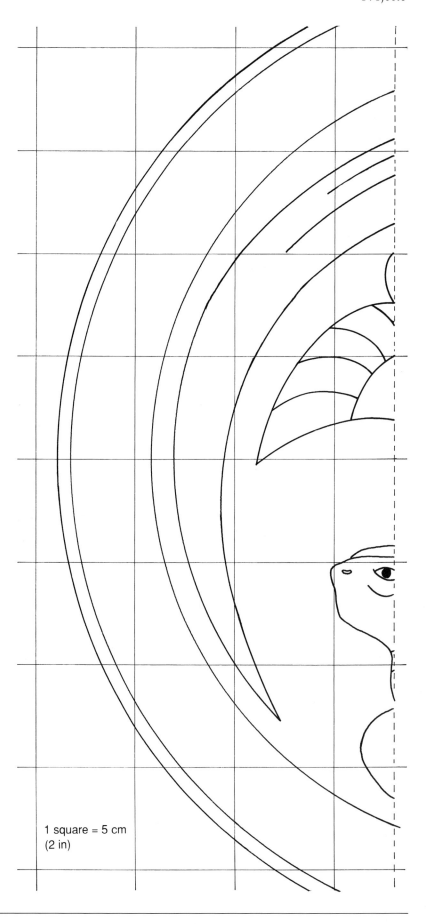

1 square = 5 cm
(2 in)

Wallhanging

Houou (Phoenix)

You will need

Top fabric: 60 × 90 cm
   (23½ × 35½ in) print
Backing fabric: 60 × 90 cm
   (23½ × 35½ in) calico
Lining fabric: 60 × 90 cm
   (23½ × 35½ in)
Reverse-appliqué fabric:
   70 × 90 cm (27½ × 35½ in)
   black (eye), 40 × 50 cm
   (15¾ × 19¾ in) pale green
   (leaves)
Patchwork and appliqué fabric:
   20 × 50 cm (8 × 19¾ in)
   deep yellow (body),
   10 × 60 cm (4 × 23½ in)
   light yellow (leaves),
   10 × 40 cm (4 × 15¾ in)
   ivory (face and wings),
   10 × 40 cm (4 × 15¾ in)
   mauve (head and wings),
   10 × 40 cm (4 × 15¾ in)
   purple (back and wings),
   20 × 40 cm (8 × 15¾ in)
   pink-brown (body)
Wadding: 10 × 10 cm
   (4 × 4 in), 70 g (2 oz)
   weight
Anchor stranded cotton: 76
   (tail), 97 (tendril), 305
   (leaves)

Finished size of wallhanging:
   83 × 55 cm (32½ × 21½ in)

Method

(See chart overleaf)
First work the curved branch of
leaves in reverse appliqué (see
pages 15-16).

Make up the bird's wings in
patchwork (see page 16).
Transfer the other shapes to
the relevant-coloured fabrics,
allowing a 5 mm (¼ in) seam all
round each shape.

Position all the shapes on the
reverse-appliqué oval, with a
layer of wadding under the head
of the phoenix. Appliqué in
place (see page 15).

Embroider the leaf tendrils
which the bird holds in its beak
and its curling tail feathers in
chain stitch, and the yellow
leaves and the line on its tail in
double running stitch.

Appliqué the finished panel in
the centre of the printed fabric.
Make up the wallhanging,
following the instructions
for the *Tsuru to kame*
wallhanging (see page 108).

1 square = 5 cm (2 in)

Wallhanging

Kabekake (Pine tree, wistaria and waves)

You will need

Top fabric: 50 × 60 cm
   (19¾ × 23½ in) off-white
Appliqué (pine tree) *and reverse-
   appliqué* (waves and wistaria)
   fabric: 30 × 60 cm
   (11¾ × 23½ in) purple,
   30 × 40 cm (11¾ × 15¾ in)
   indigo, 30 × 60 cm
   (11¾ × 23½ in) print
Backing fabric: 50 × 60 cm
   (19¾ × 23½ in) calico
Lining fabric: 50 × 60 cm
   (19¾ × 23½ in) pale blue
Anchor stranded cotton: 390
   (waves)

Finished size of wallhanging:
   42 × 53 cm (16½ × 21 in)

1 square = 5 cm (2 in)

Method

Cut the off-white top fabric into four equal pieces (fold in half and in half again). Cut the purple and print fabrics in half.

Transfer the designs to the relevant fabrics (see page 11), allowing a 5 mm (¼ in) seam all round each shape, and cut out. Position on the top fabric as indicated. Work the pine tree in appliqué and the waves and wistaria in reverse appliqué (see pages 15-16). Embroider some of the waves, as shown, in chain stitch.

With RS together, join the four rectangles to make one panel. Make up the wall-hanging, following the instructions for the *Tsuru to kame* wallhanging (see page 108).

Appendix
Japanese decorative knots

Agemaki knot

Allow 60 cm (23½ in) of cord for each knot. (See overleaf for instructions.)

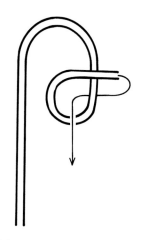 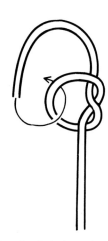 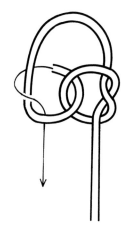

1. Fold the length of cord in half. Take the right-hand half and make a clockwise loop, as shown

2. Take the left-hand half of the cord through the loop.

3. Now take the left-hand cord under, over and under itself, as shown.

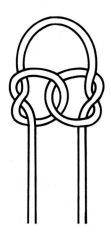 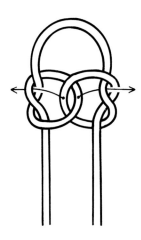 

4. Both sides should now look the same.

5. Insert your fingers through the crossed cords and pull outwards.

6. Make sure all the loops are the same size, then tighten the knot by pulling evenly on the three loops and the loose ends of the cord.

7. The finished knot.

Butterfly button and buttonhole

Allow 1 m (39½ in) of cord for each button and 90 cm (35½ in) for each buttonhole.

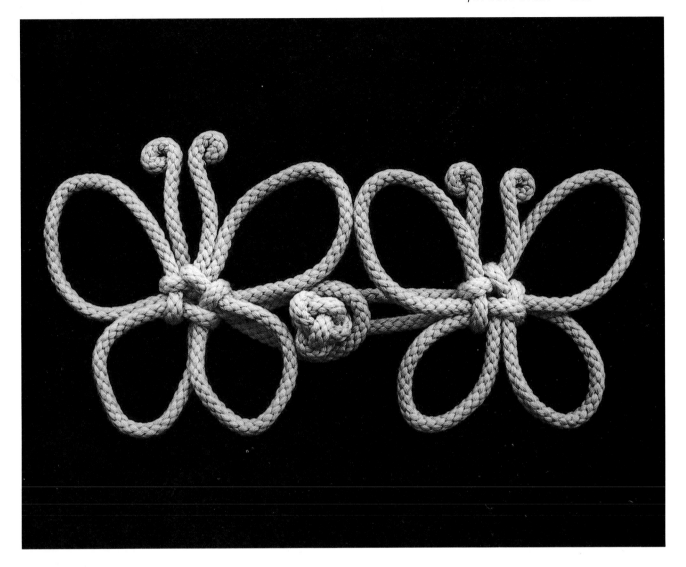

1. Make a loop in the cord.

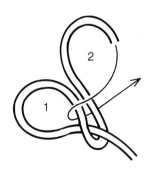

2. Make a second loop, as shown.

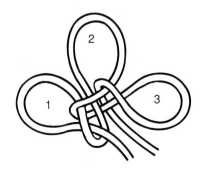

3. Make a third loop in the same way.

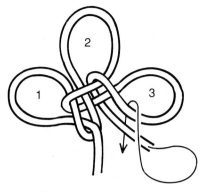

4. Make a fourth loop in the same way.

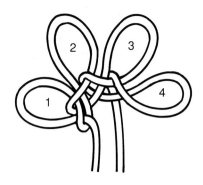

5. Turn the knot over.

6. Take the left-hand end of the cord and pass it through the opposite loop.

7. Thread the cord through the loop.

8. Turn the knot over again. Thread the same end of the cord back through the small loop illustrated.

9. The knot should now look like this.

10. Take the left-hand end of the cord and thread it through the same small loop, to make a fifth large loop.

11. Turn the knot over once again.

12. Tighten the knot by pulling evenly on all five loops and on both ends of the cord.

To complete the button

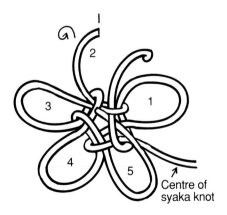

Centre of
syaka knot

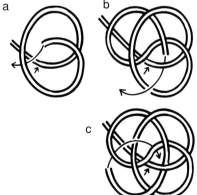

a b

c

1. To make the antennae, cut the second loop of the butterfly in half to make two equal lengths. Bind the ends tightly with thread.

2. Make a *syaka* knot as shown in diagrams *a*, *b* and *c*, leaving long ends to the cord. Tighten into a knot.

3. Sew the ends of the cord together, then cut off the surplus cord.

To complete the buttonhole

1. To make the antennae, cut the fourth loop of the butterfly in half to make two equal lengths. Bind the very ends of the cord tightly with thread.

2. Make a long rouleau loop, to hold the button. Sew the ends of the loop together, then cut off the surplus cord

Making a tassel

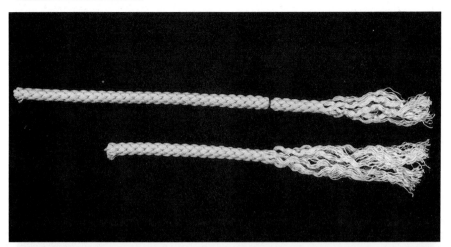

1. Decide how long you wish the finished tassel to be. Wind thread round the cord at this point and fasten securely. Fray out the strands of the cord as far as the thread.

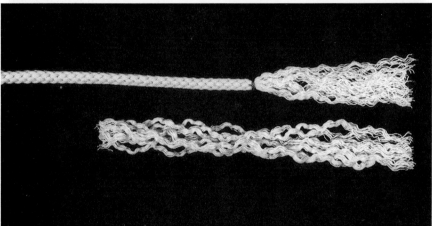

2. Cut another piece of cord twice the length of the finished tassel. Fray the entire length, using a ballpoint needle.

Wash both the frayed end of the cord and the separate frayed strands.

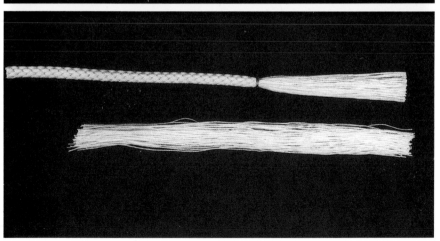

3. Comb and then iron the strands. (They may stretch in length.)

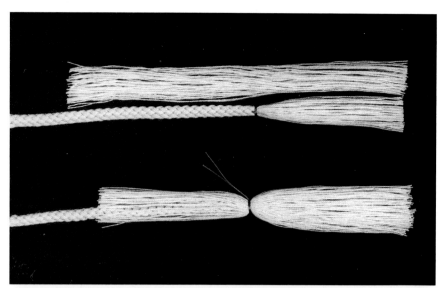

4. Take the separate set of strands and cover the frayed ends of the cord so that the core of the tassel is hidden. Tie a piece of thread around the tassel at the same point as before and tie tightly.

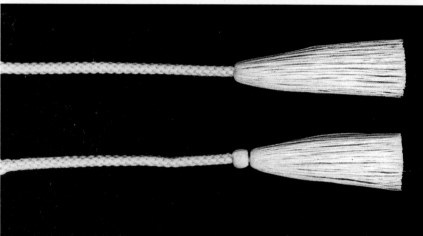

5. Fold the upper half of the threads back to increase the size of the tassel. Tie in place with thread, pulling it very tight. With a sewing needle, hide the end of the thread in the centre of the tassel.

Comb the tassel and trim the ends level. For a perfect tassel, place it on a narrow piece of tissue paper. Stick the tassel to the tissue paper with adhesive tape, and then cut a straight line with sharp scissors.

Index